UNRAVELING YOUR KNOT BALL OF SH!T

REWRITING NEURO PATHWAYS THROUGH EMDR AND MUSIC

MJ NICHOLSON

Wilder Moon Creative

WildeMoon Creative Publishing
&
in omnia paratus publishing

www.inomniaparatuspublishing.com

www.WildeMoonCreative.com

in the United States of America

ISBN 979-8-9870447-6-6 (hardcover)
ISBN 979-8-9870447-8-0 (paperback)
ISBN 979-8-9870447-9-7 (ebook/digital)

This book is dedicated to my loving partner JMC. Without your loving support and encouragement I would have never reached this point. Thank you for being the best cheerleader ever. A Ghra you are my safe harbor and I love you.

To my Children, NDC, TAWC, MERC, SMLC, LBC, & FMC you are my reason, my why, my motivation. I choose to do & be my best for you. I choose to grow & evolve to be better for you. I love you more than I could ever explain. My only hope is you all know how truly amazing you are & how proud I am of you.

NC, EP, and ERC you hold my heart, always. I love you.

INTRODUCTION

*Y*ou know those self-help books that start their introduction with something like, "Five years ago, I was a mess, my life was flipped upside down, and I changed it all with a simple trick that I will show you in this 200+ page book that I could have written in less than twenty pages. I will also have you believe that very minimal effort will go into changing what is likely *decades* of mental garbage. *And* because it requires minimal effort, this whole process should take you, like, a week, tops, before you're a mega-millionaire who is happily and lavishly living the life of your dreams. All this and more (to include a magic genie from a lamp) can be found between these pages."

IF THIS IS what you expect from this book, *stop*, close the cover, and put it down because, quite frankly, you will be sorely disappointed if you want someone to blow the rainbow farts of "super easy methods" your way.

. . .

THE HUMAN BRAIN is the single most complicated thing on the planet. Period. *Full stop.*

BUT THERE *ARE* things we can do to help ourselves heal and evolve from likely decades of mental junk, which makes us feel like crap a lot of the time.

TO ANSWER the question before it's asked, yes, I still feel like crap sometimes. I still have body issues, I still have worth issues in terms of being a wife and mother, I am still a control freak on things, and I am still trying to make my parents proud.

I am no millionaire; I am not even a thousandaire. I am just like *you*. I work very ungodly hours because the money is good, I cuss, sometimes I drink too much wine, sometimes I yell at my kids out of frustration, and sometimes I sit in the bathroom for a few extra minutes to get some damned peace and quiet.

Most days, I don't have the faintest idea what I am doing or if I am doing it right. I seem to be overly critical of myself; I love my children, husband, family, and tribe *fiercely* (seriously, I will cut you if you hurt them), and I know deep down in my soul that there is a hurt, something I can't quite reach, but I know it's there. I keep getting similar life lessons over and over, and I don't think it's just a string of Murphy's Law or that I was born unlucky, (in fact if you look at all of the things I have survived in this life, you'd think I was one of the luckiest people in the world) but it still remains an itch I can't scratch. I can't quite put my finger on it (hence the remaining issues), but I know it's there.

. . .

THIS "SOMETHING" is hard to explain, and it's like there is a piece missing. It feels like life "should" be easy, but I don't have that switch turned on. Like if I turned on the switch, everything would illuminate like the movies when everything just kind of comes into focus and the characters know all the things at once.

I HAVE STRUGGLED with this all my adult life, and if I am candid, as far back as I can remember. There is a saying—every family has a black sheep. Well, I am the black sheep of the black sheep, so I've never really quite fit in with my family anyway. But inside, internally, on a soul level, from about middle school on, I knew I'd lost something very important, and I needed to get it back.

I have read so many self-help books over the years to "fix" something I can't even identify let alone put my finger on. I've spent so much money on programs, coaches, and clinics that touted they would help me find my lost inner child/spark/passion/zing/bliss/whatever. And still nothing. That was me, foolishly thinking that it was something external that I was "missing" from myself. Like a freaking plug-and-play program, once I found the right one...BAM...life would be ahhh-freaking-mazing, and all the issues would melt away like butter on a baked potato.

AND EVERY ONE of those books, coaches, programs, and clinics had me feeling great for a while...then life happens, and I stop whatever tasks they have in the routine, and I am beating myself up for not following through, not being good enough, or not being worthy of change. Right back to the beginning, I would plummet, and I would stay stagnant in my hole of crap and wallow in what I was comfortable with.

I was comfortable in the fear; I was comfortable being the martyr and falling on my sword; I was comfortable being the victim because that is what I'd been my entire life. I wore it like a badge of honor, all the crap that had happened *to* me and so, like a comfortable pair of old shoes, it was just too easy to slip back into my crap hole.

FOR CLOSE TO THREE DECADES, I struggled with this. The forward two steps and then back five steps momentum that seemed to be my life. I hated it. It took such a toll on me physically, emotionally, mentally. It made me doubt everything I tried, did, and who I was at the very core.

Every time the five-step spot would slap me down I would fall back into that crap hole and wallow. It was easier in there, and it was comfortable because every time I fell back in that hole, it would get bigger end deeper, easier to fall into and harder to get out of.

I REMEMBER TEXTING my BBFF (best boy friend forever...yes, I know that's childish...no, I don't care what you think) about the crap hole I was currently sitting in at the moment. He gave me some very sound advice—"You can always carve some stairs into the wall to climb out. It won't be easy, but you can do it, and if you can't, I'll come down and help you."

THAT SHOOK me like nothing before...honestly.

MY WHOLE LIFE, I was the one who sacrificed everything, including myself, for others' happiness. I don't do this out of obligation but out of love. I love them so fiercely that there is no limit that has been met—yet—that I won't go to for them.

I NEVER FELT the return of that, though.

I ALWAYS FELT like an afterthought for people. Being the black sheep of the black sheep, it felt like I didn't need or deserve someone to come down in my crap hole and just sit with me and give me their time, love, understanding, and help. Like I wasn't worthy of someone's time, love, understanding, and help. Like I had to do something to prove my worth to have someone want to metaphorically get down in the mud with me and help me, carry me, love me.

AND YET HERE WAS A PERSON, one of my people, one of those I have *chosen* to be in my tribe, one I would die or kill for, one I would move heaven and earth for, and he...would do the same for me. He showed me through his words and actions that he was willing to get down in my crap hole with me, even though it would affect him negatively, and just be with me until I found the strength to build stairs to climb out again.

HE SHOWED me that I am worth it.
     And what's even better...
     I believed it.

NEVER IN MY LIFE BEFORE, not in thirty-six years, had anyone made me feel like I am worth their time, effort, energy, and love without first needing something from me. Whether it was an expectation, a repayment, or silence, makes no difference. I was expected to sacrifice something in order to receive love, help, or effort from others.

So, I went on with my life, thankful to my friend for helping me but also asking the Universe to give me something. There had to be a better way that I just wasn't seeing. I was already going to therapy once a week, and the day of and maybe the day after therapy I felt great then BAM...five steps back crept in, and I ended up still feeling like crud 98% of the time because I "just can't even" with life. Like there was nothing wrong with my life per se, but man did it *feel* like I just wasn't *enough* for anything in my life.

Not a good enough friend, not a good enough mother, not a good enough wife, not good enough at keeping house, using my skills, or owning a business. I watched others in *envy* that life seemed to happen with them guiding the wheel, and *I* was stuck holding the leftovers the Universe couldn't figure out what to do with. I have a beautiful home, a loving husband, wonderful children, a great time making money, a creative outlet that I enjoy, an insatiable thirst for knowledge, and my tribe of humans who I was lucky enough to find...there was nothing *wrong* with my life, there was something *wrong* with the way I perceived myself in my own life.

AND THEN IT HAPPENED...

IN LATE 2017, it was cold, my husband was gone as his job often calls him away, and I took his truck to therapy. It was two-fold. I wanted to feel closer to him, but he also had heated seats. After my therapy session, I was leaving my therapist's office and slid into the truck, thinking maybe I'd stop and treat myself to a flavored coffee of the season that I love, and the first song beats started to play on the radio. I knew this song. The lyrics escaped my lips without thought, feeling every inch of the words sung in places I thought were long closed, and immediately tears began to roll down my cheeks. Cursing my sensitive nature, I frantically swiped at the tears, willing my eyes to stay dry so I could drive home without

being a danger to myself or others. Nothing worked; the tears continued; I couldn't help but sing along even though the song filled me with equal parts anger, sadness, helplessness, and defeat.

THERE IS nothing unique or special about the lyrics of this song; it didn't win a Grammy, and it isn't particularly critically acclaimed; however, for me, it was significant.

The lyrics portrayed where my life was ten-ish years ago so perfectly. Every feeling and situation could have been my life. It was like the song writer had hidden cameras in my life and brain and plucked out those images for this song. Everything I could never say but wanted to, every haunting note, it was my life. And even now, about ten years later, I *feel* them with an intensity that feels like it's happening today. The feelings course through me, and with me unable to stop the tide, I hold on, helpless once again, but this time, I am powerless against myself.

SO WHY, after ten-ish years, did this song still make me cry instantly? Why did this song bring back all the feelings of ten-ish years ago like they were happening now?

. . .

THE SIMPLE ANSWER is that music amplifies the experience of the memory. It makes it richer, more vibrant, clearer, and music is also a trigger to release that memory into the "re-live now" space that typically, you can ignore or avoid.

This "re-live now" space (which we will go more in-depth with later, I promise) happens when we have decided to hold on to a memory in such a way that it actually *shapes* the decisions of now. It sounds much more complicated than it is, I promise. We hold onto these "re-live now" memories in the hopes of better enhancing our current life.

Say, for example, you have a wonderful memory at a restaurant; you will hold on to that in the "re-live now" even if you have a bad experience there later. You will "re-live" the positive until another similar "positive" comes from the same place. You will make excuses for any negative experiences you have with a positive memory, like "maybe they are short-staffed today," "It's like a new cook back there," and so on, until a new positive reinforcement comes or the negative outweighs the past positive.

What happens if this is a negative experience, though? What about, say, a car accident? Such a trauma likely initiated "re-live now" to store the memory. You likely don't like driving on the road where the accident happened, or you avoid it altogether. Maybe you avoid driving next to a type of car, or only drive in one lane. Maybe you avoid the freeway now or just one freeway. There are tons of possibilities that your brain could have come up with to keep you safe. Your "re-live now" is helping you shape the current from past events.

. . .

THIS HAPPENS with a lot of things. Does the smell of pine forest bring back specific memories? What about baking bread? When I ask you what fall means to you, what are the first words that pop in your mind? Have you ever been to a place where you have happy memories from the past, and when you revisit, you experience a calming, happy feeling? This is the same thing, except we swap the place for music.

MUSIC IS NOTHING NEW; it's been around for as long as we have any sort of history to refer to. Our knowledge of the brain, however, is an ever-evolving pursuit, and we are just starting to understand the connections we create and carry with us. Music can be used to invoke our cultural heritage, nationality, and a feeling of camaraderie at sporting events. As technology evolves, we can experience a wider variety of music from a greater range of artists. As such, we are exposed to various emotional stimuli that may apply to our current situation. This means we can hear the angst, the problems, or the joys of everyday people and connect with them in a way we previously would never have had the opportunity to.

PERHAPS YOU HAVE HAD a moment where a piece of music will give you goosebumps almost instantly, or maybe you were having a terrible day, so you turned on your favorite angry music and let that anger flow through you.

We use music in a multitude of ways to comfort, energize, release stress, or express joy. Most people use music to "pump up" for gym or training workouts or to do household chores to.

. . .

EXCITING THINGS HAPPEN when we use music to convey our emotions and experiences in life. One of the main things that happen is we further construct the neural pathways in our brain (we will get more to those in Chapter 1) as we add another sensory element to our emotion.

For example, suppose you experience a terrible breakup and throw on some rage music. In that case, you are now feeling the loss but also telling your brain that rage is the expected emotion when you get sad, thereby solidifying a pattern of behavior. Right or wrong, good or bad, these behavior patterns follow you until you actively take steps to change them. Sometimes they are harder to break than others, as you may very well find out.

Can you imagine being at a protest where discord is heavy, and music is playing? Their angst, anger, hints of sadness, and calls for change playing to a backdrop of music that amplifies those feelings. That sea of people is now one moving body, all linked with the same feelings and let's face it, "We Shall Overcome" is going to elicit a very different response from, say, "Killing in the Name Of" by Rage Against the Machine.

Ever see someone crying as their presidential candidate won? Do you ever pay attention to the music? What about watching a video of a "mob mentality"? What kind of music do they import as the background track? Have you ever watched a scary movie and noticed the suspense-building crescendos used, and perhaps you've noticed your heart skipping a few beats with the music. These are all examples of how music can affect your emotions on a larger scale. Can you imagine what effects it can have when you have no influencers other than your mind?

. . .

WHEN MUSIC IS PLAYED, and someone has an attached emotional significance to the music, we experience these emotional responses that create physical symptoms within a person. For example, we may experience goosebumps which is a physical response to an emotion that we are feeling from the music. Ever feel your heart beat faster when you listen to your "rage" music or a piece that is particularly suspenseful? These are actual physical responses our body creates from music, something we listen to and our brain interprets. Most musical pieces are between three and five minutes long, so our brains make a rather informed decision on whether or not to create a physical response pretty quickly. Typically, we don't just add music to memories all willy-nilly. Normally, our brain deciphers the lyrics and delivers the meaning to us before "layering" that music to our memory. Sometimes we make this decision on the first pass. We hear the song, listen to the lyrics, and feel the significance. Sometimes we make the connection after hearing the song a few times or more. There are exceptions to this, though. For example, suppose the experience is particularly emotional or significant, such as a birth, death, or a wedding. In that case, the connection is made in a surprisingly short amount of time in the grand scheme of things.

I WAS BORN in the '80s and grew up in the '90s, so I grew up in the era of grunge rock, and although I was raised listening to the sounds of Led Zeppelin, Pink Floyd, and some very fabulous 80's big hair bands, I slid right into loving grunge. Some of the beats were OK, but it wasn't the head banging, waffle shirt, Doc Martin, bomber jacket wearing ideals I liked. It was the lyrics I could *feel* as real as the problems in my own life. They are filled with angst against society, parents, and life because we felt we had the wrong end of this

11

deal, and our music perpetuated this raw anger and rage so well for us. When we had something not go right in our life, we turned on our music as loud as it would go, and we felt a connection...somebody, somewhere out there, "got us." They understood our life, and we were heard. These lyrics poured

through our speakers that spoke of our life, that "knew" us, eliciting an emotional response, whether reaffirming our anger or giving us peace that someone understood us. We linked an emotional connection to the feelings we were experiencing through music.

EVEN IN THE MID-1700s, people found the connection between music and the soul.

Voltaire stated, "Poetry is the music of the soul, and, above all, of great and feeling souls."

We could go even further back too...Plato, anyone?

Plato advised, "Music gives a soul to the Universe, wings to the mind, flight to the imagination, and life to everything."

AND THAT SIMPLE theory is the basis of this book. How we, the emotional creatures we are, have found a way to layer memories (either good or bad) into the furthest reaches of our mind with additional emotional and external

stimuli. And believe me, we will get into this *way* in-depth, but I just wanted to give you an idea of what exactly this book is about.

THE JIST, essentially, is that we all have a knot ball of shit, every one of us. Some of us were given tools to help with the untying of knots, and some of us were not made aware of knots let alone that we had to untie them. We struggle to "fix" ourselves (you are not broken...stop that crap) but continuously seem to take one step forward and two steps back. I'm here to tell you that unless you unravel the center of your knot ball of shit, you will always be doing a two-step with yourself. But (of course, there is a but...come on), you have *no way of knowing* what the center of your knot ball is.

REPEAT THAT WITH ME, "I have *no way of knowing* what the center of my knot ball is."

SO, here is the crux of the issue. We continue trying to fix something unseeable and unknowable, but we can recognize that something is "off." We don't know what the issue is, but we can often see the most recent layer of the knot ball, so we start to unravel that. Huzzah! We see some progress, we feel *great*, then we take a step back to give some room for all this new awesomeness...and step right into the previous layer...and repeat a mistake we thought we fixed...well, crap.

NOW I FEEL LIKE A FAILURE, I can't keep my life on track, and I'm back to visiting "life sucks" town in my crap hole of shit.

Sound remotely familiar?

If so, keep on reading, as this book may be able to help you get to the center of your knot ball. If not, you are an unnatural weirdo...kidding, but this book may give you some new insights, too. So, keep reading...weirdo.

THIS BOOK CAN BE helpful to everyone, mainly because I write exactly how I like to talk to people and how I would want someone to talk to me when trying to understand a complex subject.

So, if you were expecting a literary masterpiece or a university level text, you will be sadly disappointed.

If you like people to give it to you like it is, in a fairly no-nonsense manner, then, man, have you picked up the right book.

If you are one of those individuals who react "more" (goosebumps, tears, anger) to music, this book will be highly beneficial for you (whether or not you like my writing style) because the method in this book specifically deals with the multiple sensory tags (ie, music) that are attached to your memories.

YOU WILL HAVE exercises to help you discover the center of your knot ball. I implore you not to skip those. I know homework sucks, and I hate doing it too, but it will make your process that much easier if you play along. So, buckle up; you're in for some interesting things.

WHAT'S GOING ON IN THAT
NOODLE OF YOURS?

If you want to find the secrets of the Universe, think in terms of energy, frequency, and vibration. ~ Nikola Tesla

The brain is such an interesting thing. It can complete things on its own. We don't even need to think about it. Our brains protect us from the mundane (ever get home driving the same route you've driven a million times before and once at home have to actually think about how you got there because you do not remember?) or the traumatic. They even have the ability to transform how we experience our world.

Now I know that last point has you stopping in your tracks...transform worlds...ugh. This is another 'change your thinking, change your life' book, isn't it?" No, it's not. In fact, this is the only time you'll ever hear this from me, so listen closely. Changing your life through thoughts IS possible; it's just science. Like attracts like, therefore if you are expending positive energy into the world, you are creating space for positive energy in your life...SUPER SIMPLE. The main downfall with 99% of books that tout the ability to change your life through thoughts is that they are missing a critical part, the part of the action that is crucial to changing your life. Positive thoughts and energy plus positive actions equals positive effects. Did you really think you could sit on your butt and wish for the perfect mate to come into your life without leaving the house? But this is another topic for a whole other book... (which I will likely write soon), so back to the brain.

The brain can do some pretty amazing things, and it's one of the most complex things in our universe. Frankly, we know squat when it comes to the brain and its potential.

So, first things first, let's discuss what I lovingly refer to as your "knot ball of shit."

That's right...you have a knot ball of shit that keeps rapping you in the ankles all the time, just so you don't forget it's there.

What is your knot ball of shit?

In the simplest terms, your knot ball got formed in the earliest stages of life before you could actually remember and has continued to grow with every event that reaffirms the "truth" your brain knows. Sounds super easy to fix, right? Yeah, nope.

Now stop for a second and use your imagination...humor me. Imagine you're three years old. You love to watch Barney, Sesame Street, or maybe some Mickey Mouse. You listen to music that your parents play, you love to play with your toys and outside in the dirt and grass, and you are super curious about your world. You also know that the mommy person keeps you fed and mostly happy. The daddy person you don't see very much, and when you try to play with him, he often pushes you away, and he "doesn't have time" for you. You have someone called "brother," who is sometimes nice and sometimes mean, and sometimes when he's mean, he makes you cry. That mommy person is the only one who really loves you.

What do you think this three-year-old version of yourself would think, regardless of whether or not you have memories of it?

Likely, it would look something like this—"Daddy doesn't want me. Brother says I'm a pest. He's mean to me, makes me cry, and I need to leave him alone," and "Mommy loves me."

Logically, as adults, we can come up with a wide variety of reasons we would never hold onto this damaging information. However, as a three-year-old, we don't run on logic, and our brain sees "daddy doesn't want me" as critical information to be saved. So, the brain does what it does—saves this information and processes it as fact. Every subsequent time that "daddy doesn't want me," we are reaffirming the negative neuro thought, and the brain again does what it does and further cements this information. As you get older, you then apply this "fact" that you have been nurturing in your brain for years to other situations that don't involve your father. Your girlfriend dumped you, so "she doesn't want me." You get picked last for team sports, so "they don't want me." Your job let you go, so "they don't want me." Your dog ran away, so "even Fido doesn't want me." Whether it is actual reality or your perceived reality through the lens of "they don't want me," you reaffirm the thought of "they don't want me" over and over. What started as your three-year-old mind making an observation (the center of your knot ball) has now evolved into your entire life (each incident is a new layer on the knot ball), and this is why many people don't see a marked, *permanent* difference when they try to make changes in their lives. You unravel the top layer of your knot ball of shit, but your knot ball will find its stride again and start knocking at your heels.

See the complexity and importance of this "knot ball of shit"?

The only way to unravel the knot ball is to find its center, which is not an easy task.

I don't remember much from when I was three years old. I mean, I have a cool scar on my forehead and a story that was told to me, but I don't actively remember this. Now when we acknowledge that these memories that form the knot ball of shit can happen at two, one, or even in utero, we can begin to see that we are not going to have an active memory of this.

And I know what you're thinking, "In utero?!?!

Yes, new studies have shown that babies in utero can pick up negative energy (Ugh...why can't this be a girl, why did I sleep with such a lowlife, my partner is so distant—maybe she is leaving with the baby...etc., etc., etc.), since fetuses in utero have fully functioning auditory systems around twenty weeks old. This can, in fact, form the center of the knot ball. When you add in that all of our other senses are dulled, our eyes are functioning, but we are in the dark womb, our touch works, but we can only feel ourself, our taste works well, but we can only taste amniotic fluid, our smell works but...fluid, and our hearing also works...and man does it work. Plus, we do know that sound travels *so much* better in water, right? And while we were getting ready to bust into the world, we were effectively swimming in water, so forming the center of the knot ball in utero is not a far reach at all.

So, how do we unravel something we can't even remember? How can we get to something that the brain hides from us?

Oh, yes...the brain, that tricky, tricky thing.

Once the brain decides something is "true," it is permanent, and our brain holds onto that information as vital, super important stuff. Then, once it determines that something is damaging to us, it hides it, like it's super classified information and only one person is ever allowed to see it and in order to keep it super classified, we also go the extra mile and hide it from anyone and everyone (including ourselves), so no one can use this super classified information to hurt us.

So, what happens when the brain decides something is super damaging to us, perhaps even traumatic in our young, naive perception?

The brain deems this information too damaging and hides it not only from us but from itself. Tricky, tricky...right?

Now think again, like a three-year-old, would Dad not wanting us be important and damaging information?

Yes.

So, the brain did what it does, hiding this information from itself for fear of hurting us. Yet we continue on with life, thinking, "What is wrong with me that no one wants me," which, in fact, causes more damage.

Not only that, but it's also reinforcing what the brain took as truth, further solidifying this as a fact of life for you. So, you are continuing to perpetuate this cycle of shit, with life constantly reaffirming what your brain is telling and has told you is truth your entire life.

So, to put that simply, whatever the center of your knot ball is, your brain (although it keeps this information from you) looks for every opportunity to keep you safe from this damaging information. It will look for every instance that looks like "daddy doesn't want me" and apply the "daddy doesn't want me" narrative to it, thus keeping you safe from it while simultaneously reminding you of it all the time.

It kind of makes sense, right?

Of course, it does.

Why else do you think Sally in apartment 2-B keeps picking the same kind of guy? Or Tom from work can never move out of middle management?

We have been cultivating the same experiences with

different characters our entire lives. Even successful people hold this knotted ball of shit; they aren't immune. You can have a successful business but be on your fourth marriage with children who would rather you fall off the face of a cliff. You can have a loving family and a successful business but have severe body issues and self-hate.

So, this should be an easy fix, right? I mean, this is just finding the knot ball and unraveling it.

Unfortunately, it's not that simple. Remember, the brain is complex.

Imagine your brain is a series of interrelated freeways. When you start a new job, hobby, diet, way of life...whatever, your brain creates a small one-lane country road after you have jumped from a frivolous, fly-by-night thing to a solid habit, which happens around roughly fourteen to twenty-one days of participating in the habit regularly. Each time you participate in this task after that point, your one-lane country road becomes bigger, wider, deeper, thicker, stronger. So, it jumps from a one-lane road to a two-lane road, then a four-lane highway, then six, then eight, and pretty soon, you're cruising along on an eighteen-lane super-highway, and this habit is so ingrained it's like second nature.

Let's use English as an example. As a baby, you knew nothing of English. Those people who fed you and cared for you sounded like the teacher from Peanuts. Slowly, you gained a better understanding of what the words meant, then you learned to speak the language, then read it, then write it, and now it's second nature. You don't think about how to form words or sentences anymore because it's one of the oldest superhighways in your brain.

These superhighways are built with both positive habits and feelings *and* negative ones.

Now let's think about this in terms of your knot ball of shit.

The first time your brain stored "daddy doesn't want me" as fact, you built a one-lane road, then it grew bigger each time you experienced a feeling of "they don't want me." Each time you reaffirm that center of your knot ball, your brain says, "See, I told you I was right," and subsequently adds a new lane until it's a superhighway. When it reaches super-highway status, or eighteen lanes wide, your brain keeps adding on layers of new concrete to make this eighteen-lane superhighway as strong as possible. After all, we don't want some schmuck to come and topple this beautiful piece of engineering, right?

Now you can see the complex system of superhighways running through your brain, everything from your love of piano to "they don't want me." You are constantly reinforcing existing superhighways or creating new ones every day. That new yoga class you fell in love with and signed up for classes four times a week? That's a new one-lane road. You recently found out you have gluten intolerance and have to change your eating habits—this is a new one-lane road. Everything that you take to and past the habit stage (roughly fourteen to twenty-one days), is creating a new potential superhighway.

If all it takes is the habit stage to create a new one-lane road and we can change our lives, why can't we see change on a more permanent and consistent basis?

Remember that knot ball of shit? That's why.

We have been running on the "they don't want me" super-highway our entire lives. It's a mega superhighway, eighteen lanes wide and a ton of layers deep. When trying to run a one-lane road against it, we, of course, fall back onto the quickest route we are comfortable with when faced with an issue that reaffirms our old patterns.

If we run into frustration or let down in our lives, the brain wants to immediately default to something it knows, not something it has to try to remember. That eighteen-lane superhighway is pretty darn established at this moment and is *so* easy to get onto with all of those on-ramps.

We travel down that one-lane road, and we are feeling pretty darn good about our decision to start this new whatever. We took off the top layer off our knot ball and decided we deserve/want/need better than that pattern we have been so comfortable with forever. Because we took the top layer off our knot ball with our decision to change and our subsequent actions related to the change, that knot ball loses some of its balance because you removed the top layer. It's no longer in stride with you, knocking at your heels at every opportunity. Then...*then*... the knot ball finds your stride again (you shook it off for a little while...good job) and knocks you back onto the mega superhighway. The one-lane road becomes neglected and overgrown from disuse because you're back on the mega superhighway, and eventually, it's like it was never there at all. This cycle repeats itself over and over, with you unknowing about what is going on and with your brain continuing the pattern of protecting you from what it feels is most damaging.

So, let's look at a real-life example. Food. More specifically, desserts. If you are/were a good girl or boy, you got a treat. We carried this mindset into adulthood, so when we want to feel good, we get ourselves a treat because we want to be a good girl or boy. When we start a new diet, we go into it with gusto. We are doing great, drinking more water, cutting calories, carbs, sugars, (whatever the case may be), and we are *cruising* down that single lane dirt road. Then something happens. A stressful work deadline, or maybe we hit a plateau with our weight loss. Smething happens, anything that we would have normally turned to food to help us feel better about, and our brain looks for the easiest way to make us feel better, like a good boy or girl. Before we know it, we are buying that pint of Ben and Jerry's to make us feel good, and we are right back on the superhighway we were working so hard to get off of. At the same time, our brain says, "See, this ice cream makes us feel good, doesn't it," until reality sets in that we failed on our mission to get ourselves healthy, and we beat ourselves up for reaching for the spoon. We are now stuck in the shame/soothe spiral until we shake ourselves out of it again and try once more to get healthy, but by now, that one-lane dirt road we started is overgrown with barely an inkling there was a road there at all, and we start all over again.

It's kind of easy to see it when it's broken down like this, right? It's easier to see the pattern we continue to repeat and why we have some change that we feel good about and then get slammed back into our old patterns.

Now, I know what you're thinking. You think this means you cannot institute consistent change in your life.

And you're wrong.

You can change your life and the behaviors that continually creep up in your life; it all depends on how hard you try and your level of dedication to you.

Will it take work?

Absolutely.

Will it be easy?

Absolutely not.

Will it work if you keep at it?

Absolutely!

That's part of the beauty and mastery of the brain. It's constantly rewriting the ongoing narrative that runs in your mind (think of this as a background program on your computer that is constantly running) to best fit the needs of the human at any given time. The easiest analogy I can think of is when the brain changes your narrative almost instantly (for most people...I know there are those exceptions to everything...including this) when you find out you're going to be a parent and then actually becoming a parent. For the majority of your life until that point, you had yourself to worry about; that was the narrative that your brain ran. Then you find out you or your partner is expecting a new life that you helped to create and planned for together. Your brain instantly switches narratives to begin planning for the little bundle and to make changes in your lifestyle for this new life. It is no longer just you, or you and your partner, to worry about, it's all of you. There is no waiting period. It's not one of those "well, let's see what happens in four to six weeks" or "let's make this a habit" kind of things. It is an instantaneous thing that happens once the brain realizes this is a new life for you and the new narrative begins. It changes almost instantly again once the baby is born. This tiny human is now your number one priority; its very survival depends on you to make it so. The brain doesn't need time to make these changes; it just does it automatically and as efficiently as possible. The narrative is rewritten in an instant in order to meet the new demands you've given it.

This is why I internally laugh when people tell me they need time to make the adjustments. No, you don't, or rather your brain doesn't. You—logical, analytical, overthinking you needs time. Your brain? Nah, it can handle things in an instant. Just think if you were never told by anyone—I am talking television, movies, magazines, books, family, friends, the old lady at the supermarket, the well-meaning bloke at work, *anyone*—that "good things take time," "anything worth anything is worth the wait," and on and on that goes, would your brain believe that things can change in an instant or that things take time? I'm willing to put the $20 in my wallet on the fact that if you were never told that things take time, you would change things in an instant because that's how the brain works.

So, what's different between rewriting the narrative for

having a baby and rewriting a narrative for making positive changes in your life? A lot, actually, and none of it really benefits you. Remember when we were talking about the brain processing information as "fact" and "truth" from your own early stages of forming self-perception, whether that was in the womb or anytime before five-ish? Well, a baby (especially one who is wanted and planned for) is seen as "fact" and "truth." You will have to change your life when you become a parent. We've witnessed this in our own lives, through our friends, and through society, so the brain takes this information, "your life will change when you have children," and stores it as truth.

For our own self-perception, we've already stored what we know as "truth" and "fact" from an early age, and we have been lovingly building on it ever since. So, trying to impart a "non-truth"/"non-factual" information stream that cannot be verified by society/environment/friends/or really anyone other than our moms (moms will forever tell you that you are awesome, and frankly, we think they are lying or they have to say it because, you know, they are our moms), is detected right away as it goes against the set current narrative and is dismissed entirely. So, if the information you have is that your life and lifestyle will change after having children, then your brain sees this as truth and adjusts accordingly. You can't give it a falsehood about something it has deemed "truth."

So, why can't we just change the "truth" our brain knows as "fact"? Good question. And I have a good answer.

It would be *super awesome* if it worked that way. Do you remember when we talked about the brain hiding traumatic/hurtful/bad things from us and registering certain things as "truth?"

Remember, the brain is super complex. We essentially

have three parts of the brain that you need to concern your-self with.

**The peons who carry out the rote motions and actions.

**The manager who tells the peons what to do and the only one who talks to the CEO.

**The CEO who carries all the information we have garnered as important, facts, truths that we have learned throughout our lives.

Now the peons can't really talk to the CEO to tell the CEO that this is now fact or we need to do this. The only one who can do this is the manager, but the manager is a douche sometimes and doesn't take all information received to the CEO.

Why would he?

I mean, he can't go running to the CEO every time a peon comes to him with a new idea; the manager has to filter what the CEO receives. The manager does this by running the new information against what we already know as truth or fact, and the manager got that list directly from the CEO. If it doesn't align with what we already know as truth or fact, then it is discarded, and it never reaches the CEO. After all, the CEO already told the manager what it wants by way of what is truth or fact...so why on earth would the manager give the CEO something it doesn't want?

That, my friends, is a great way to get fired.

The sad reality is, if our "truth" was not a positive one, and we try to implement a positive one now, the brain says, "Now see here, hoss. I know full well that *that* is a lie. Don't you bring that malarky in here again!"

Let's take a look at this from our "they don't want me" narrative.

We go our entire life with our "they don't want me" idea, the knot ball growing larger each time we reaffirm this narrative. From Dad to our girlfriend, to our dog, to the job we didn't get, we have subconsciously said, "this is truth," "this is our life," and "we need to continue on this path." When we make a positive plan that we are going to change, we say, "I'm going after that new job, I am overqualified, and I know I'd be good at it, I'm going for it." The manager takes this information and says, "No, this doesn't go with the narrative the CEO has directed. This is going straight in the recycle bin." Now, we may get the new job, but it may not be exactly as described. I've been there. A job sounded fantastic, a social media expert for a new start-up. Yeah, they wanted a house manager with less than 5% of the job being as described. Whatever the case may be, we will find a way to fill the narrative that the CEO has put forth.

So, how on earth do we get the manager to relay life-changing information to the CEO?

Well, we tell him the truth...of course.

If the manager only wants to hear the truth, you give him the truth...or what he can only see as truth, so he passes the information on to the CEO.

For example, we *know* that exercise helps us stay healthy, regardless of if we *like* exercise. We know exercise helps us maintain good health. If we try telling our brain, "I love to exercise," the manager says, "This is a lie, so it goes straight to the recycle bin." If we slightly alter our statement to, "I love being healthy," the manager can't say, "this is a lie," because this is true. No one enjoys being unhealthy, so this new statement is fact, and our subconscious will attach what we also know as fact to our statement of fact about being healthy. So, it would look like this. "I love being healthy (truth)," "healthy means exercise (truth the brain already knows)," "Healthy means eating good for me foods (truth the brain already knows)," "healthy means drinking water, (truth the brain already knows)," and this goes on and on. Once the manager submits a "truth" or "fact" statement, the CEO works to attach all of the subsequent "truths" and "facts" to the new "truth" so they are all one long line of "truths" or "facts" about the topic in question.

Now, is the manager going to accept this as truth on the first go-around? Likely not. Odds are you will have to make an active effort many times a day for twenty-one-ish days (habit-forming days), repeating the same truth for the manager to finally get it. If you add action into your truth-telling (ie, taking the stairs instead of the elevator while saying, "I love being healthy"), your manager takes you, your words, and your actions a little more seriously.

Not as complicated as some make it out to be, right? Once you know about what's going on and how we can change it, that, my friends, is half the battle. But sadly, most of us walk blissfully unaware of what is happening in our brains with little to no recourse to make a substantial change in our lives. We continue to choose the wrong men, the wrong job, live life eking out a meager existence with blips of happiness, never truly knowing what it means to find joy in work because "work wasn't made to be fun" and "nothing worth having comes easy" or better still, "there are three things in life that are unavoidable—work, death, and taxes." We use phrases like, "it's just how it is," "I've always been late," "if I even look at cake the wrong way, I gain ten pounds," "I've had a hard time nailing down what I want," "I always put my foot in my mouth," "I never win anything," "I'm not," "I can't," and "I'll never." All of these negative thoughts just reaffirm the "knot ball of shit," and you will continue to pack on pounds, work in an unfulfilling career, or just live life the way it always has been.

Making a conscious effort to direct your thoughts away from the superhighway of shit you've been traveling on is a good start, but how do we *find* the superhighway of shit? I mean, most of us have more than a handful of issues, so how do we find the one that is the center of it all, especially when we likely cannot remember it?

Good question, grasshopper... You're learning.

Follow me to a truly magical place that will change your life....

Kidding! But it is pretty interesting.

THE CONNECTIONS THE BRAIN
MAKES WITH MUSIC

"**G**iven that music preferences are uniquely individualized phenomena and that music can vary in acoustic complexity and the presence or absence of lyrics, the consistency of our results was unexpected," the researchers wrote in the journal *Nature Scientific Reports* (Aug. 28, 2014). "These findings may explain why comparable emotional and mental states can be experienced by people listening to music that differs as widely as Beethoven and Eminem." (2-1)

Before I get into anything else, we need to go over what music does to the brain and how our brains respond to music. Which in and of itself *should* be very telling of the link that music makes for us.

Scientists have studied and researched the heck out of this connection, and man, it is really cool how your brain will "light up" or "shut down" depending on what you're listening to.

That's one of the things Jonathan Burdette, M.D., has found in researching music's effects on the brain.

"Music is primal. It affects all of us, but in very personal, unique ways," said Burdette, a neuroradiologist at Wake Forest Baptist Medical Center. "Your interaction with music is different than mine, but it's still powerful.

"Your brain has a reaction when you like or don't like something, including music. We've been able to take some baby steps into seeing that, and 'dislike' looks different than 'like' and much different than 'favorite.'" (2-2)

For me, this part is really fun; I get to tell you all about the connections the brain makes with music (and other external stimuli), how the brain then interprets these connections, and how it affects your life. For me, the hours of research, the countless hours I have spent speaking to many professors, are worth it all because this is where it all kind of comes together.

Dr. Joe Dispenza said it amazingly well, "Our research has shown that a clear intention, (which is an act of a focused and coherent mind), coupled with an elevated emotion like joy, gratitude, care, wholeness, freedom, and compassion (which is a function of the heart), changes people's states of being. Music is the necessary component of the process." (2-2)

"Music is the necessary component of the process."

When we want to "be" happy and hold onto "elevated emotion" like joy, care, or freedom, the easiest road to get there is music.

And history proves this theory correct as well.

Literally, for as far back as we have written history, we have music. Furthermore, it doesn't matter what culture or region you are in, there is music. From the biggest city in the world to the most remote village of people with no outside influence, there is music, beats, words sung or spoken in rhythm.

The sounds of war drums beating sent soldiers into the

mindset of one hive fighting off an enemy instead of fighting off an enemy as individuals.

Nursery rhymes and lullabies hummed or sang to soothe a crying tiny human or beast.

Disney gave us "whistle while you work" and "in every job that must be done, there is an element of fun" while singing to the children.

We have seen the signs and know the vitally critical part music plays in pretty much our whole lives. We were just painfully oblivious to it most of (if not all of) the time.

Music and the attachments/intertwining/influence it creates in our lives are in the background. It's like a background program on your computer. It's running without your input, knowledge, or even conscious thought, and although it plays an important part in shaping what we think and how we react, it is really a background program that runs without us actively thinking about it.

I mean, who really pays that much attention to the background programs running? On my computer, I have to actively go looking for them. They are called background programs for a reason. Who has time to sit down and evaluate every single background program that are running?

So, are you really that surprised that we have some sort of connection between our memories and music?

I mean, when I started my research, after my "Einstein-like moment" crying in my car, it was like the logical side of my brain was saying, "well, DUHHHH, I thought everyone knew this."

*exacerbated side-eye at logic. "No, I obviously didn't."

So, what does science say about music and our brain? Surprisingly, a lot. There have been many studies on the subject, and some are currently ongoing. So, I am glad you asked because I am about to lay it all out for you.

Music can engage the brain in four key ways, of which

three are really important to us, so we will focus more on those.

First is emotion, which, if we are honest, is really no surprise. Emotion links us all in everything we do. From loving the smell of freshly laundered clothes or hating our job, emotion reads on us like a novella. Studies have been done on our emotions and music, and through these studies, we have garnered that music stimulates emotions through certain and specific brain circuits. (8-2). Research further shows that music (more specifically singing) can release other beneficial things like oxytocin and dopamine.

So, when you are belting out the tunes to your favorite rage music, you are releasing *feel good chemicals to an angry reaction.* Anyone want to guess what happens to the neuropathways when this happens? Likewise, when you are singing along with some happy, feel-good tunes, you are releasing feel good chemicals in your brain to a happy, feel-good feeling.

As we briefly touched on how music is woven through every facet of our lives, from our first kiss at the middle school dance to watching our children walk down the aisle to the wedding march, our emotions are there, right alongside the music.

We all have music we turn on when we are angry or sad, just like we have those "I love this song" moments that we need to crank it up as high as we can and often will turn on specific music when we want to reinforce the specific emotion we are experiencing. For example, we are not likely to blast romantic love songs on the way to the gym, we are likely going to play music that pumps us up, so we can get into workout mode.

Next, we have memory (I bet you see where this is going now, right?), and if you've ever spent any time with a person suffering from memory loss or dementia, you can certainly attest that even if they forget everything else, they still "love that song" and can likely remember most if not all of the words. If you've never experienced this firsthand, you can go volunteer at a senior center or just trust me. At the time of this writing, I actually have a friend in Canada who is doing an informal study with music and Alzheimer's patients.

Studies have been done, most notably, a 2009 study from Petr Janata with the University of California at Davis, in which he specifically linked that the music we connect to on an emotional level can also connect us with deep, meaningful, and sometimes hidden memories of our past.

This is where your personal playlists will come into play. The songs that are on that playlist hold specific emotional significance to you, and they have the ability to unlock the hidden and meaningful memories that your brain is holding as truth. Think of those carefully curated playlists you have. I personally have eight playlists that are meticulously created for the specific mood I may be in.

The songs of significance from our past will continue to hold significance in our present and future unless a deliberate separation is made between the music and the emotion.

Neuroplasticity and learning come next, and you may be saying, "MJ, what in the dear sweet bread and butter pickles is neuroplasticity." And that is totally OK. Before I learned what it is and why it's important, I would just shake my head and nod like I knew what they were talking about. So, I've got you, and I'll explain it.

Neuroplasticity is essentially the brain's ability to create those mega superhighways from one-lane country roads. Neuroplasticity also comes into play when there is damage or injury to the brain and it finds a new pathway to still function. If you break your right hand, your brain has to quickly move dominance from right to left, so you can still complete daily tasks. Neuroplasticity helps with this.

Music has been played for patients with moderate to severe brain injuries, and through this music, they were able to reconnect to personal memories.

I want you to stop and think about that. Patients with brain injuries, who maybe were unable to recall certain parts of their life, were able to make connections from listening to music that they had an emotional connection to.

Lastly, we have attention, which isn't super important to what we are doing, but I'll include it for your reference. And really, this is pretty self-explanatory; some people show greater attention to tasks and learning when they are listening to music. Many studies have been done on this subject, with perhaps the most notable ones done by Stanford University School of Medicine.

In one study, they learned that it is through the pauses between musical changes that our brains are actually firing on more cylinders, so to speak.

This is also why some people actually learn better when listening to music or singing the information in the form of a song.

I'll let you in on a little secret.

I could never remember the order of the planets. It was one of those things where I was struggling to remember the names of the planets themselves, let alone what order they went in.

And then I had kids, and my kid happened to love the show *Blue's Clues*. In one episode of the show, they went to space. While in space, Steve and Blue learned a song about the planets from the sun, and now, twenty-something years later, that is the only way I remember the order of the planets; I seriously sing the planet song from *Blue's Clues*.

* * *

ENGAGING the brain is important for us to understand because if we can understand why the brain engages emotions to certain kinds of music, we can try to alter the effects.

Each person is different in their musical tastes. However, there are key components that we will get to in another chapter, like the heightened suspense music they play in movies to prepare the watcher for either a big scene or another suspenseful scene. So, we are basing this work on what would be the key musical cues that people seem to generally respond to. It is important to note if you do not respond to such a musical or emotional cue, then you would need to do a little digging to find your own, but I am here to help you with that too.

You're going to do a lot of that work. This isn't just an "I'm going to tell you what to do and leave you on your own to figure this s#it out" kind of book.

This is more of an "I'm going to tell you exactly what to do, and we will do some homework exercises together to find the individual answer that resonates with you" situation. I will be holding your hand through this.

And as we will find when we do these exercises, we make intricate connections with music, and these connections go on to shape what we think, feel, and do.

We make these specific connections with certain music mainly due to environmental structures placed in our formative years.

Yep, when you're a little bitty baby (maybe even in the womb), your brain is making connections to music.

So, for example, if your parents only listened to Buddy Holly, you likely have a strong affinity or dislike, depending on your childhood experience, for Buddy Holly. This can be used for any genre, artist, or period of music. Even if there was no music in our childhood, we have peer and societal musical cues that give us direction. Examples of this would be the happy music that commercials play, and you visually see happy people, and your brain links the two. Even if you don't listen to "bubble gum pop," you've likely heard of it and immediately link it to overly exaggerated happiness. The same can be said for death metal; we instantly link that to unhappy, angry people, who may be trying to steal our souls, but they could, in reality, be some of the kindest people we meet.

These societal interpretations are everywhere with every genre of music, even slogans, commercials, jingles, and TV show intros.

These environmental cues are ingrained within our brain thanks in part to the visual cues that we get from society and our peers.

We can hear something and create imagery based on what we already know about that subject from what we have heard from others, society, or the media.

I know, it's kind of confusing. But trust me, you do it every day, all the time, without even knowing it.

"In countries such as Germany," Burdette noted, "music therapy is commonly an integral part of the rehabilitation process for people who have had strokes, brain surgery, or traumatic brain injuries.

"If you're trying to restore neuroplasticity in the brain, to re-establish some of the connections that were there before the injury, music can be a big help, and I'd like to see it used more widely in this country," Burdette stated.

Burdette is also a proponent of programs that help people with Alzheimer's, dementia, and other cognitive and physical problems that reconnect the individual with the world through music. One such program is Music & Memory, which employs iPods with customized playlists featuring songs popular when the participating individual was under thirty years old.

"You can actually see the power of music," Burdette said. "People who were just sitting there, not engaged in anything, light up when they start hearing music from when they were 25." (8-3)

* * *

WE ALL HAVE this relationship with music. This invisible partnership with music that our brain is fully aware of and responds to in a variety of ways. Music can help us study better, make us smarter, have a better relationship with ourselves and others, give contextual clues on what is happening around us, make us angry, or make us happy. It is entrenched in every area of our lives from birth to death.

So, now that we kind of know what music does, let's explore how we can use it to help ourselves. Right now, it's like background programming running, and not only did we not know it was there, we didn't even know what it does and how it affects our lives.

But now we do.

THE BRAIN, EMDR...WHAT IN THE WHAT IS THIS STUFF ALL ABOUT? LET'S DISCUSS THE NUTS AND BOLTS OF IT.

*I*f you need or want to know more about EMDR, how it works in the brain, and all the other brain-related stuff, then this chapter is for you. I will break everything down, so it is understandable and digestible so you can better understand who, what, when, why, and where. If you don't give two squirts of piss about how it works, just that it works, feel free to skip this chapter. Reading through this chapter to get the benefits of this book is unnecessary, so this section is optional and up to you. However, if you really want to jump further into EMDR, please look up Dr. Francine Shapiro, who is quite literally the pioneer in this field, and we will get into her breakthroughs a little later in this chapter.

HOWEVER, assuming you're still with me and you're vaguely interested in learning about EMDR, let's go through the very basics of it.

. . .

Neural Pathways

Let's start in the simplest way, with neural pathways. In the simplest terms, these are our brain's way of passing notes in class.

A neuron is a nerve cell that transmits signals to and from the brain, and the route/road/highway that these nerve cells use to get the information to and from the brain is just called a pathway.

So, what are these neural pathways for?

Do you remember when I was telling you about those superhighways we build and how they get broader and more profound the more we use them? And how when we are on the superhighways, we can create a new one-lane country road to change a pattern, habit, or belief, but it is pretty easy to get bumped back onto that mega superhighway?

These are neural pathways.

We create them from childhood and nurture them until we die.

They can be beneficial to things such as learning a language. When we are born, we don't have language skills; we cry, and that's it. But now, after so many years of nurturing that neural pathway, reading and writing in your native language is second nature; you don't even think about it. You don't have to.

We learned long ago in childhood that touching a hot stove will burn our fingers, so we created a neural pathway for hot, fire, and burning, which has kept us safe our entire lives.

WE ALSO CREATE LESS universal neural pathways that are more individualized to our unique upbringing. You may have learned from a very young age that you don't sit in Grandma's special chair unless it's your birthday because it's literally called the birthday chair. This makes your day more special and unique, and you have a fondness for the chair.

WE MAY ALSO HAVE pathways that are linked to a favorite food, texture, or place from our childhood that we can find traces of today. From picking your honeymoon spot based on your love of trees to your favorite comfort meal being tacos.

**PSSST...THESE are real-life things for me, in my life, my personal pathways.

THIS IS ALSO true for negative interactions.

HAVE you ever stopped to ponder why you hate public speaking? Did someone tell you that you are a "jabber jaw" and need to learn to be quiet? Perhaps you've built on that your whole life only to now have a crippling fear of public speaking.

. . .

CAN YOU RECALL GETTING A "TREAT" when you've been good? Maybe you were a "good boy" and ate all your dinner and were rewarded with ice cream, and your brain interprets that as being good; feeling good with sweet or fatty foods. Now, when trying desperately to feel good, you may overindulge and eat a pint or two of Ben and Jerry's.

THE TRUTH IS your brain only knows what you've given it for information, and sadly, many of us (nor our well-meaning caregivers, for that matter) understood the complexities of this.

THESE NEURAL PATHWAYS (mega superhighways) serve us in every facet of life. Now, when we change our neural pathway into that one-lane, bumpy country road, we are taking into account the other neural pathways that we have built to reinforce our mega superhighway.

IT SOUNDS SUPER COMPLICATED, I know. I'm over here trying to tell you that your brain is an intricate web of stored and borrowed knowledge, and your brain will try to find anything similar to make corresponding roads to support the initial roads. So, let's take a real-life example so we can gain a better understanding of how exactly this works and what it looks like to us.

WE WILL TAKE GETTING in shape, for example. We know that getting in shape is good for us, exercise is good for us, and being healthy is good for us. We also know that "I must be disciplined," "I have to work hard," "exercising is tiring," and "exercising is boring." Literally all the positive and negative statements you can attach. They can be vague because it's what you've learned through media or friends, or it can be individualized to us because it happened specifically to us or is something we actually witnessed. (This can also mean witnessed on social media...I'm looking at you, gym shamers!) These supporting roads support both our positive and negative main roads simultaneously.

ALL OF THOSE sub-neural supporting pathways prevent an actual change in the "get a gym membership and get healthy" mindset because we still have these negative highways when trying to attach a positive highway.

TO BREAK THIS DOWN FURTHER...

1. NEURAL PATHWAY saying I want to get in shape

2. SUBSEQUENT NEURAL pathways stating exercise is good for us, exercise is healthy

3. SUBSEQUENT NEGATIVE neural pathways stating exercise is hard, exercise is boring, exercise is time-consuming

WHILE THERE ARE two positive pathways that are leading to positive change, there is one subsequent neural pathway that is staunchly against change and will fight like hell in order to keep the status quo. Not only that but the negative sub-neural pathway deals with and affects other pathways as well. Time-consuming, costs, commute, etc. That one negative sub-neural pathway connects to other negative neural pathways.

I KNOW, right?

THIS IS why we need to work at the core of the issue instead of pulling at random strings to exact the change we desire to see in our lives. When we start pulling at random strings, we have no idea what they are attached to. The working theory is that by rewriting the entire knot ball from the center, it will also remove all the subsequent threads hanging around. This will allow you to go to the gym using number one and number two with no negative number three hanging over your head, threatening to sabotage you.

ADAPTIVE INFORMATION PROCESSING **Model**

THE ADAPTIVE INFORMATION Processing model is essentially a theory of how the brain works.

TRADITIONALLY SPEAKING, the brain was previously thought to take incoming information and process that against vital statistics, such as is this a threat, is this food, is this care. We use all of our sensory organs, including sight, sound, taste, and touch, to give information to the brain so that it can decode and store the information that is needed. Once the information is decoded, the brain sends it to the garbage bin, sensory storage, working storage, or long-term storage. It has long been thought that once the information is stored in long-term memory, those memories have to be brought out from "deep storage" by way of specific stimuli that prompt memory retrieval. This prompt can be as simple as looking at pictures from your wedding day or going through old toys you saved from your children's childhood. Given this model, it is hard for others to understand how and why repetitious actions persist in an individual's life when there's no background; this traditional model does not allow past shit to influence current shit.

Now, with the Adaptive Information Processing model (or AIP for short), we have a completely different theory on the brain's working, processing, and storage of memory. With AIP, the theory is that trauma (the center of your knot ball of shit, that three-year-old stuff you thought was totally life-changing and needed information to set as "truth") is processed but not stored. When new experiences similar to the initial trauma occur in an individual's life, they are pasted into the existing memory network that was never stored correctly. It's essentially always adding to this memory. It isn't "one and done," as the traditional model states; it is always adding onto the initial memory with current instances.

I EXPLAINED this earlier as a camera filter, which is probably the aptest description I can give it.

WHEN THIS INFORMATION does not get stored properly, it becomes a camera "truth filter." When new incoming events happen that are similar in nature or that contain truths that we have tied into the filter, we automatically apply the "truth filter" to this event. This event then goes through the processing, sorting, and memory storage as it should; however, once it is processed, sorted, and in memory storage, it further solidifies the "truth" of the original filter and makes the neural pathways stronger.

So, instead of just being an unrelated memory that we simply process and then move on, as the traditional model states, we actually have a super complex web of filters and storage that interconnects everything. When we are in a new situation or experience that we have not personally been in before, our brain does some fancy maneuvering (there is a whole chapter on this, Chapter 6, so I promise I won't leave you hanging without this information) and pulls experiences that it has seen before but never personally experienced.

When we look at the AIP model, it will look more like interconnecting roads all coming from or going to specific memory points on your neural pathways. Pulling information from specific memory points in which the brain already has a history or knowledge. Those neural pathways are really the end-all and be-all in terms of memory storage, function, and new information sorting and storage. And when the new incoming information does not get sorted correctly (it now has that camera "truth filter" on it from the previous memory), the brain takes the filtered information as "truth."

Ah, yes...those neural pathways, that's right. Everything you accept as truth and put into memory storage makes those neural pathways (ie, your mega superhighway of shit) wider, deeper, and stronger. This infographic is perhaps one of the best I've seen to describe the AIP model.

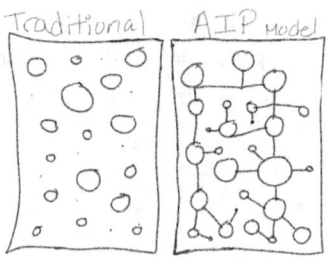

IT SHOWS the left side as many think of the brain, with many unconnected events and thoughts just rolling around solo up there, waiting for you to grab onto one. On the right, it shows how everything is interconnected and how one seemingly insignificant thing can be the start of this entire web of experience that is currently your reality.

I KNOW ALL the pieces are falling together, and an internal "ah-ha" may be happening...pssssssttt

I want to tell you a secret...

This is a good thing, I promise.

COGNITIVE PATTERN RECOGNITION

COGNITIVE PATTERN RECOGNITION reinforces the Adaptive Information Processing model. It is essentially the brain looking for patterns in everything and matching that with the information retrieved from somewhere in the mind.

Experts believe this was initially developed by our caveman ancestors to keep themselves alive. If caveman Bob heard or watched caveman Steve get attacked by a predator from the bushes but did not retain this information, the next time caveman Bob heard a rustling in the bushes, he did not react to the rustling; it would be bye-bye caveman Bob if there were a predator making that rustling instead of the wind. Instead, caveman Bob retained the information and filed it under "Important." When he heard the rustling again, he used cognitive pattern recognition to determine that he should probably be wary, at the very least, of the rustling.

WHEN INCOMING INFORMATION IS RECEIVED, the brain automatically filters through short-term and long-term memory to recognize similar details and compares the received information and the known information.

A WIDE VARIETY of cognitive pattern recognition subcategories work along the same lines; one good example is Pareidolia, which is finding a face on or in inanimate objects, such as the Man on the Moon or the Beyoncé Dorito.

COGNITIVE PATTERN RECOGNITION goes by template matching, prototype matching, feature analysis, and top-down and bottom-up processing. Individually, these are all similar yet unique enough for me to briefly explain them.

TEMPLATE MATCHING
Template matching is perhaps what most humans use

when they're doing cognitive pattern recognition. It essentially states everything is stored as a rough template, and when we encounter anything similar to the rough template, we apply that to this new information. This basically means everything we see, do, or have contact with, we only understand based on past exposure, and when we encounter something new, we must create a new template on which to base future encounters.

PROTOTYPE MATCHING

PROTOTYPE MATCHING IS BASED on the theory of a general prototype instead of an exact template. So, for example, if we see A, B, and C, we do not see the individual letter templates. We see the alphabet prototype and put all letters that we know from English into this category. If we see a fox, we can arrange that into a more generalized prototype category for canines or into an exact template for foxes.

FEATURE ANALYSIS

FEATURE ANALYSIS WORKS on the premise of recognizing multiple patterns at the same time. It is at its base allowing all incoming stimuli to simultaneously be filtered in, and then the brain picks out key features in order to make sense of this incoming information. For feature analysis, this would be akin to your wedding day—there's a lot of incoming data, and if your brain went to store all sensory input from your big day, it would likely have a short circuit somewhere. So, it takes all of the incoming sensory information, picks up key features, like your wedding song, walking down the aisle, and maybe the taste of cake, and files those instead of the entire sensory input.

TOP-DOWN AND BOTTOM-UP *Processing*

EVEN THOUGH I linked these in the same category, they are, in fact, two separate entities.

TOP-DOWN PROCESSING IS USING background information in the brain to recognize the pattern. It's typically working with the person's knowledge of a previous event similar to the current one and then making a prediction of what is going to happen based on previous event knowledge. So, this is like Tommy and Sally have been together for six years, and Tommy knows Sally has a wandering eye when he doesn't pay enough attention to her. Based on Tommy's previous experience and knowledge of Sally, he knows that the likelihood of her wandering eye, since he has been working lots of overtime lately, is high.

BOTTOM-UP PROCESSING IS USED like data processing. We take facts based on our environment, not just our knowledge, for our perceived knowledge and make a prediction based on environmental-based facts. Say, for example, we know when the weather gets colder in the winter months, we need to turn on the heat in the house. If we don't turn on the heat in the house, we will likely freeze. So, environmental-based fact tells us to turn on the heat, so we don't die.

· · ·

So, in terms of cognitive pattern recognition, there are a lot of variables that come into play that'll lead us (or rather our brain) to form conclusions about situations, feelings, and things that we do based on the AIP model, and even if we discard the AIP model, the cognitive pattern recognition cycles lead us to select events which reinforce whatever negative or positive highway we have chosen.

EMDR

EMDR, Eye Movement Desensitization and Reprocessing Therapy, was the brainchild of Dr. Francine Shapiro, who developed the theory in the late 1980s. Essentially, Dr. Shapiro recognized that rhythmic eye movements could reduce the intensity and frequency of disturbing events/memories/feelings. She worked hard to refine her theory and, in 1989, conducted a study to document EMDR therapy and the results. Dr. Shapiro published her findings in the *Journal of Traumatic Stress* which showed marked improvements (therefore a success) in victims of trauma.

In the beginning, a patient would sit relaxed and watch a lighted panel. The lights would cycle from left to right in a comfortable pattern for the patient. Some patients, like me, prefer a more rapid approach to the movements, and some prefer a slower pace; it's all about the patient's comfort level for maximum effectiveness. Once the patient is comfortable, a series of questions are asked to guide the patient through the mincfield of trauma.

Now, I am going to pause right here and explain the word guided because I know some of you are like, "they were messing with their minds." And the answer to that is no. By guided, I mean a clinician asks the patient to go to a safe space, and only after the patient is ready does the clinician bring into play the questions of feelings/emotions/ memories that were brought up in previous sessions. Mind you that the patient is always asked what they want to work on today, and it is never left up to the clinician; this is a patient-driven therapy. The clinician decides the best way to get to the patient's desired outcome and directs the conversation based on the patient's wants, needs, and responses. So, for example, when I was in therapy, I told my clinician that I wanted to work on feeling worthy (yes, in case you were not yet aware, I see a therapist...this is not a bad thing) because for as long as I could remember at that point in my life, I had never felt worthy of anything, including love. I went to my happy/safe space, and we plunged when I was ready. My clinician started by telling me to take myself to the place where I first felt unworthy; my mind went to being a crying baby in a crib. The alone that I felt was immeasurable. It was all-encompassing and everything. The clinician then asked me what I felt: frightened, alone, and empty. Like I knew that somehow this crying child would be ignored, left to cry, and remain unwanted. It was such an ugly feeling, and we took that road. My clinician directed each new feeling or image that would come to me and that I would express. That particular session left me feeling exhausted and drained. This is what guided means in this instance. The clinician is simply making the patient focus on one aspect of the imagery or feeling.

BACK TO EMDR. Once the patient has processed enough information through the session, the clinician brings the patient back to a safe place, and then they work through this newly discovered information. The clinician also walks the patient through safer techniques for redirection and positivity in order to start a positive knot ball instead of rebuilding the negative one they are trying so hard to remove from existence. EMDR sessions typically last an hour or so, with the patient only dealing with the brain for about thirty or so minutes.

IT WOULD BE amazing if we could just jump in and tackle all of the unwanted/bad shit in our brain at one time, but it would not be advisable. Your brain has worked really, really hard for years, maybe even decades, to store, hide, cultivate, and keep track of these "truths." It needs a little bit of time to process this newly empty space and fill it with something else. (Remember that sentence. We will be saying it again and again, but that is stupid important, so remember it.) Therefore, I would never advise anyone to attempt to do more than one treatment per week.

SINCE IT BEGAN, EMDR has taken a slow and steady climb to a recognized treatment therapy for patients. It has also evolved from just eye movements on a lighted bar to vibrating paddles, earphones with a special right-left noise track, or pretty much anything that will simulate the left-to-right movement of the brain. Finding a qualified clinician in some areas is still a struggle, but if you can find one, it is worth it to check it out.

EMDR HAS DIFFERENT PHASES, and once I describe these phases to you, you'll kind of see a parallel between what we're doing in this book and the different phases of the

EMDR. Traditional EMDR works in three to eight phases, depending on the issue's severity and depth.

Phase One

Phase one includes typical patient/therapist interaction. You go into the office and explain what has been bothering you and perhaps what you would like to work on. To your best recollection, the clinician also takes a full history of any medical or mental issues and any future goals or current triggers. With this, you work together to come up with what you both think is the best place to start. In my experience, starting has been in an innocuous place that didn't really hold significance for me, and then we moved on to more in-depth experiences. This phase is always sitting with a clinician and finding out just what the problem is. This can be done in as little as one appointment, or it can take several; it all just depends on how deeply the issue is rooted. It's like when you walk into a room and forget what you went there for. You go to the therapist's office wanting to get better, but you have no idea what you're looking for in your brain, and this isn't even touching the fact that your brain is hiding things from you. Because we link things in our brain and due to the fact that when we add multiple layers of stimuli (touch, sound, taste, etc.), to memory, it becomes more pronounced in our mind, music is a very good gateway to not only our issues but a pathway into repairing them.

Phase Two

The second phase is making sure you have the tools to combat stress and obstacles in your life in the future. There is a positive way to handle stress, and there are a million and one negative ways...the negative ways have helped get you here, so we don't want you to continue those now, do we? And don't worry, we will be going over stress busters in a later chapter to help guide you away from the negative patterns and onto a healthier one. Phase two is essentially this book. In a traditional setting, the clinician would explain what EMDR is and the process of EMDR and introduce the patient to their safe space. A safe space is very important in this procedure because if the brain doesn't feel safe, it will not go down any sort of rabbit hole to find the memories to release them. If the brain feels threatened in any way, it will do what it does and hide this information from you.

Phases Three Through Six

Phases three through six are actually doing the EMDR (which I will go through a modified version of in just one minute), where we focus on the feeling or emotion (in traditional EMDR, we try to locate a visual image of the issue that is related to the memory), connect that to a negative core belief or a negative belief pattern we have about self, and lastly any related emotions or body feelings that we notice come up during or after EMDR.

PHASE THREE IS the assessment phase. This is all about finding the target memory, and what that means for us is finding the target emotion related to the memory. So, in traditional EMDR, the clinician would take you back into your safe space and then, through some leading questions (which I touched on earlier in this chapter, so you shouldn't be freaking out about it now), guide you to finding that memory or emotion that we are looking to target in this session. Once we find the target memory or emotion, it is pretty self-guided. Afterward, the clinician gently guides you to further reaches or links to those memories or emotions. Clinicians use the Validity of the Cognition Scale and/or Subjective Units of Disturbance Scale to determine how exactly that individual responds to the EMDR.

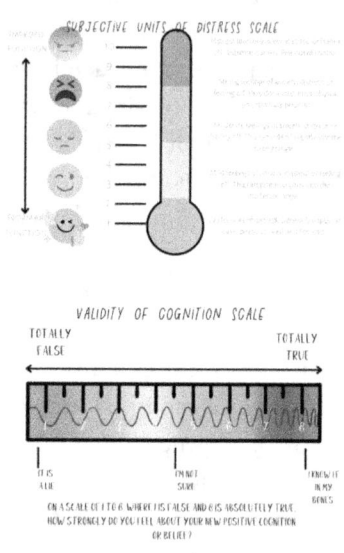

Phase four is called desensitization, which means that the individual is focusing on that memory while simultaneously focusing on either the light movement, the paddle movement, or the sound movements. Now when the individual is focusing on both this memory or emotion and the EMDR stimuli, what happens in the brain is interesting. When we are discussing EMDR and the brain, there are a few areas we kind of need to be aware of; the first one is the back of the brain which is the processing center, the second is to the right side of your ear, and this is your sorting center, and then the last one is the front of your brain where your forehead is, and this is your storage or memory. When your brain is focused on the EMDR stimuli while simultaneously holding memory or emotion in the forefront, an interesting thing happens, that memory or emotion loses some of its punch. Now, for some people, it can lose all of its punch. It's like a lion's roar looking at a kitten. But for others, it will just lose a little bit of its punch. There really is no wrong or right; it's all based on how deeply ingrained this memory or emotion is and how well you're responding to the EMDR. Again, this goes back to the Validity of the Cognition Scale and the Subjective Units of Disturbance Scale. You may want to bookmark this page to keep returning to those scales and utilize them as your benchmark for progress.

PHASE FIVE IS PRETTY important as it is the installation phase. Now, I know you are thinking, "heck is an installation phase?" and I am here to tell you. It is where you put in some positive formations of a new neural pathway because your mind is a little susceptible right now after you've cleared some space with phase 4. So, even further on in this book, there is an entire chapter on ways to positively combat your negative neural pathways. You choose any one of these (or more, you can honestly put as many in there as you want) positive pathways, and you focus on that as you're releasing some or all of the negative memory or emotion from phase four.

SEEMS SUPER SIMPLE, right? It kind of is.

SAY, for example, falling back on our old "daddy doesn't want me," instead of reaffirming that, you would now say, to yourself, out loud, however you need to, "I am wanted, I am needed, and I am loved." We are essentially hitting a positive and fighting it against this negative while simultaneously weakening the negative's power. It's like fighting the big boss from Super Mario Bros. If you keep hitting it, eventually you beat it and go to the next level. This gives the positive input a fighting chance or, better yet, an edge over a negative input, taking control all the time.

So, phase six is the body scan. Now you're probably thinking, this is like some hoodoo, voodoo, new age stuff, and I can assure you it's not. Do you guys remember when we talked about physical representation or physical manifestation of the negative properties?

I bet you do; I bet it's coming back now.

The physical representation of stress is possibly an ulcer, headaches, back pain, and on and on it goes. The reality is that we physically represent our internal struggles, so why is it so far out there that we would be able to evaluate how we are feeling physically through a body scan after we have done work like EMDR on ourselves? It's not; it's really not. So, what is the body scan? A body scan is taking stock of yourself. Sounds super simple, I know, but it is bringing awareness and noticing in the present moment where exactly you are feeling it.

Here's an example; if I had just completed an EMDR session on a relationship that was extremely toxic and violent, I would sit and notice that perhaps I was feeling some extra pressure in my throat, which is the physical representation of me feeling voiceless or that nobody would hear me if I asked for help in that situation. For a body scan, you just take notice of how you're feeling. Where are those instances of pressure, tingling, or maybe physical pain (which I have felt before, in my chest, actual physical pain), and note these down. I will include a helpful chart of how to body scan, what to look for, and how to identify what it is for you.

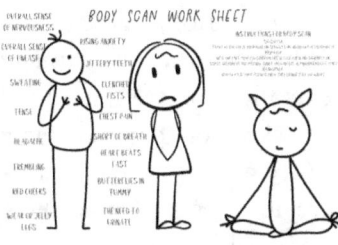

Phases Seven & Eight

Phases seven and eight are continuing care and reflection, respectively. This is where you will use those tricks and tips for managing stress and keeping a positive self-image on a daily basis. We do not want to ruin the progress made with old bad habits, so this is a very key, important part. After about a week, we take honest stock of how we are feeling, how the method using music and specific songs still affect us, and any emotional ties surrounding the music.

And then we repeat this entire process until we are done.

PHASE SEVEN IS FOR CLOSURE. Typically, the clinician brings the individual back to their safe space, grounds them with a few questions, and briefs them on what can happen in between sessions. For us, this will be a little different, and we will go more in-depth with this in (chapter __), but for right now, just know we are going to use music again...ohhh yeah. This phase allows the brain to end on a "high note" after giving it the positive formations from the installation phase or phase five. You are essentially reaffirming the positive thing that you told your brain.

PHASE EIGHT IS REEVALUATION, and normally the clinician asks the individual to keep a log/journal of any feelings, memories, or events they feel are related to the last session. (Remember when I asked you to get a composition notebook specifically for this...yeah...you need one.) You are also asked to review your previous feelings from the sessions/writing using the Validity of Cognition Scale and/or Subjective Units of Disturbance Scale. So, prior to you starting any session on yourself, you're going to evaluate how you feel on those "core feelings" that you have been writing down based on either or both scales. And then, after a session, you are going to reevaluate those feelings using the same scale you used first to grade yourself.

WHAT'S up with the left to right movement of the brain?? Why on Earth is it so freaking important? I'm glad you asked; let me explain.

The eye movements in EMDR have been hotly researched and debated for years. Some out there say that the eye movements, IE, and bilateral stimuli are unneeded and don't significantly change the treatment method. However, equally convincing arguments and research state that bilateral eye movements provide significant benefits when utilizing EMDR. Now I'm going to break this down as simply as I can because it's kind of important for you to understand and utilize when you do the work later on in the book, so I'm going to give you both sides of the story on the bilateral eye movements so that hopefully you can make the decision yourself that this would be the best course of action for what you're doing. In 2001, a meta-analysis was done of the thirty-four studies that had been conducted on EMDR over the years, and the study focused on emulating the same procedures but without the eye movement component. This specific meta-analysis showed no significant incremental benefit to the overall outcome, specifically due to the eye movements. Now it should be noted that this was conducted almost ten years ago, and our understanding and perception have changed slightly.

MORE RECENTLY, in 2009, a study was conducted using bilateral eye movements, a counting task, and no brain busy stimuli with EMDR therapy. It was shown through this study that bilateral eye movements reduced the vividness and distressed ratings the participants reported on the Validity of the Cognition Scale and or the Subjective Units of Disturbance Scale. This study goes on to say that a concurrent task that matches the individual's preferred modality successfully reduces distress when compared to two tasks that serve as distractors only.

Now what that means is that you have to give your brain busywork for it to be able to move out of the way so that you can directly affect the "film" memory that is imparting its biased view on an incoming memory, and this is, of course, based on the AIP model of the mind.

The researchers found that this busywork needs to be more specific to the individual; just like everything else in the medical world, it really isn't one-size-fits-all that will work for everybody; it is more that we know this works with success, but it would work better with greater success to tailor it to the individual.

Now, if you recall, I talked about tapping a beat on your legs, moving your eyes back and forth, listening to music one earphone at a time, or simply tapping alternating feet in a beat or pattern. This is the individual tailored modality and, working along with the trigger stimuli (whatever piece of music you decide to start with that elicits an emotional response within your "negative core emotions"), provides results more closely related to the 2009 study.

Now BACK TO EMDR. With EMDR therapy, paddles, lights, vibrations, and/or movements are key to the therapy. It is a rhythmic pattern that gets the conscious brain "quiet" for a few minutes so that you can let go of constant thought and move a layer of film you had previously held in your processing center to the sorting center and then to the appropriate place.

Remember when we talked about the three parts of the brain that you need to know for this? These are them. You have the processing center that holds the films of "truth" that overlay anything and everything that looks similar to what we "know" (remember our "truth" films never leave our processing center. They constantly and consistently cloud every event that happens in our life). There is the sorting center which filters where things go from processing. In this location, we reaffirm our truth further by not "trashing" insignificant events which should rightfully find the bin. Items get sorted into short-term and long-term memory along with vital storage and trash. Long-term storage, short-term storage, and the trash bin are the final step in this process. Most things with "film" on them never go to the bin...like ever. We hold onto those suckers for dear life because they are our "truth," even when it's damaging, even when it's harmful, even when we don't need it or want it. We save it like our life depends on it.

PLUTCHIK'S WHEEL OF EMOTIONS & Maslow's Hierarchy of Needs

Plutchik's Wheel of Emotions, Maslow's Hierarchy of Needs, and even Hawkins' Levels of Consciousness are all pretty much the same thing or at least reiterating the same thing. Robert

Plutchick has designed a three-dimensional model which explains in pretty good detail the core and secondary emotions we have touched on previously. Maslow's Hierarchy of Needs explains pretty well why people are so willing to continue with a negative path even though it does them no good. And Hawkins' Levels of Consciousness are what tie our emotional and mental states to what we are outwardly projecting into the world. A lot of information, I know. And some of that sounds like "new agey" stuff. But in reality, it is all very interconnected, so we will go through each of these and connect the dots as we go.

PLUTCHIK'S WHEEL of Emotions is just that, although sometimes it's a vortex, cone-looking thing, it looks like a big ass flower. In the center of the flower are eight core emotions, four negative and four positive, that each secondary emotion stems from. So, the basis is that all emotions can be broken down into anger, anticipation, joy, trust, fear, surprise, sadness, and disgust, and these main emotions are the catalyst to a whole host of secondary emotions, which is what we see, use, and know on a daily level. The premise of Plutchik's model is that each emotion has an equal and opposite emotion. So, the obvious opposite of joy is sadness. It bears mentioning here that this design is a cone/vortex on purpose. If left in the "anger" position, the emotions can and will intensify, sending you down the spiral/vortex/cone, which makes it harder to get back to the top.

WHEN WE DECONSTRUCT Plutchik's wheel more, the further you travel down the cone/vortex/spiral, the more intense the feelings. If the feelings are more intense, your awareness of them is heightened. The more your awareness is focused on your intense feelings, the more you try to escape them, deny them, or run away from them. The more you try to outrun them, the more they come and slap you in the face, making you notice them, which in turn continues this cycle.

Do you see how this cycle can grow a bit tiresome? You're literally running around the bottom of the vortex, skipping over some emotions and staying in your comfort zone. This is all brought to you by the lovely emotion of fear. Fear is the mother of all of them; remember, we were born with fear already ingrained in our emotional arsenal, and it is hammered into us to be fearful of damn near everything. (Don't touch that, or you'll get burned, look both ways before you cross or get run over, don't talk to strangers or get kidnapped, etc.).

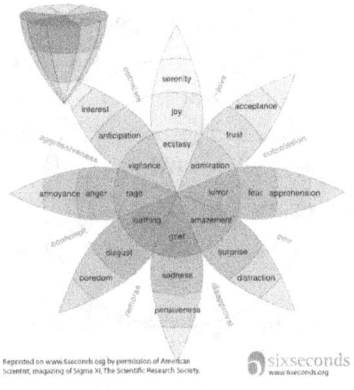

MASLOW'S HIERARCHY of Needs is a well-regarded and highly-referenced theory that is essentially a guide to human motivation. The largest layer of the pyramid shape is the physiological layer, followed by safety, love/belonging, esteem, and self-actualization.

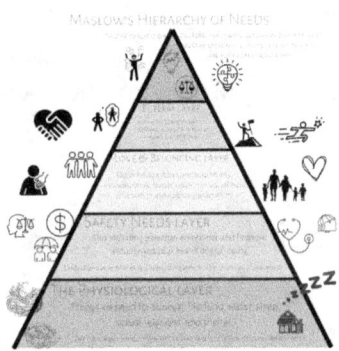

THE PHYSIOLOGICAL LAYER is made up of things we need for survival, like food, water, sleep, sexual relations, and shelter.

Let's say that one of your core negative emotions is tied to not having enough food or shelter as a child. That lack will continue to breed fear of not having or being enough your entire life, sending you further down the spiral of the wheel of emotions, never really able to gain footing.

The same can be said for safety needs, including personal, emotional, and financial security and your health or well-being.

And love/belonging is where friendships, intimacy, and family are located, with self-esteem holding the lower and higher ego, importance, recognition, respect, and self-respect.

That leaves self-actualization, which holds mate/partner acquisition, parenting, using abilities and talents, pursuing or obtaining a goal, and seeking personal happiness.

As you can probably guess, the higher you go up the pyramid, the more entangled your knots get. When you have fears about your parenting, your self-esteem will likely not be on point. You may have questions about your financial security, leading to doubts about basic needs like food and shelter.

These can all be tied into various emotions, perpetuating the cycle.

Hawkins' Levels of Consciousness is just like the other two in that it references your emotions on a scale that can be measurable.

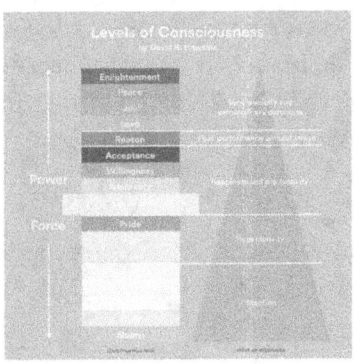

For example, you have lots of guilt in life and maybe contemplated suicide, and the levels of consciousness refer to this as a step above shame. This theory is based on linking our emotions to physical actualities that we can relate to in order to better understand where we are and where we would like to be emotionally.

So, by contrast, if you're feeling willingness, you're likely to be happy and have a heightened level of productivity.

The levels of consciousness I really use and rely on for reflection are so that we can understand that not only people but objects, events, and an entire community can even be ranked within this scale, and we can see kind of what needs to be done in order to bring ourselves into a more happy state. So, for example, if you believe that you are a hapless sinner and nothing you can do will be up to par, you will likely suffer from a lot of guilt coupled with shame and possibly apathy and anger at the entire situation. And the only real way to move forward through those feelings is to see it for what it is, accept it, process it, and move forward to a higher level and, thereby, a better state of being.

. . .

WITH ALL THREE of these models, we are focusing more on an AIP model of the brain, that past influences can affect the current state of emotional being and that those past influences affect the current perception of events.

WHAT IS the bottom line when it comes to the brain? How it works, in my opinion, is how it is being presented here.

ESSENTIALLY, our brain is a working reminder of things we have not processed, and it will continue to remind us on some level of things we need to work through. I know we've all heard the saying, "the universe keeps giving us the same lessons until we've learned," so we will keep making the same mistakes until we try a different way.

AND KUDOS to you for reading this far and giving another way a try. But I know you're ready to go. You are pumped like Ahhhnold and ready to put in the work to do this ....so let's go.

MEMORY AND REALITY

*M*emory is a fickle beast. Reality is even more so. Reality is often dependent on an individual's perception of the events as they take place, which is why two people can have two very different experiences of the same event. Each is their own reality, true to them. Most people assume that memory is stagnant and that once it's in there, it's like a brick wall and pretty unmovable. However, memories are not stagnant; they can be influenced, altered, and even entirely made up.

YES, you read that right; you can make up memories for yourself or others that never even happened.

WE OFTEN THINK of memory like a video camera that provides us with a true recall of the event, however memory is nothing like that at all. It is more like specific components, main ideas, and personal triggers...everything else about the memory...it's kinda made up.

. . .

I LIKE TO IMAGINE MEMORY/NERVOUS system like a predictive search engine. Once you start inputting, some letters possibilities start populating. Once a better picture of what you're looking for comes up, the predictions get better. The brain does pretty much the same thing. It looks for things that are similar to the information you are giving it. It gives you a bunch of scenarios based on what you provide.

MEMORY STORAGE ISN'T EXACTLY perfect either.

WHILE MEMORY STORAGE is a rather simple process, there are many moving parts to make it appear so simple.

WHEN TALKING about the mechanics of the brain, everyone pretty much knows a few key parts.

If I were to say things like "temporal lobes" and "hippocampus," you are likely nodding your head like "yuuuuup."

BUT WHAT IF I asked you what those things *do*?

CRICKETS

YUUUUUUUUP.

. . .

WE KNOW of them but literally have *no* idea what these things do.

And that's OK. I was like you too. I nodded my head, "yup, the temporal lobes are part of the brain." And then shut my mouth because I had nothing else to add to the conversation.

So, I decided to change that. I have spoken to doctors and professors, read so many books I can't even begin to tell you, and researched my tail off. I wanted to know everything I could so I could understand it better and then explain it to all of you.

So

HERE

WE

Go

THE TEMPORAL LOBES handle auditory processing *and* attach meaning to long-term memory. (I bet you're already seeing the significance of this one, huh.)

THE HIPPOCAMPI (one in each hemisphere of your brain) are a key component in forming new memories and spatial understanding.

. . .

THE AMYGDALAE (AGAIN, one for each hemisphere of your brain) assist in decision making and forming appropriate emotional responses.

THE ENTORHINAL CORTEX is located in the temporal lobes and acts as a transportation hub for spreading and retrieving memory. If your brain was a grand central station, then the entorhinal cortex is the hub directing all the trains where to go and what to do. It also serves as the main go-through for the hippocampus and the neocortex.

THE NEOCORTEX IS, in part, responsible for higher-order brain functions, such as sensory perception and cognition.

THERE ARE hundreds of parts of the brain that we can go through, one by one, detailing what they do and why they are important. However, we really only need to focus on these three. While each part of the brain is important and necessary to, well, make you, you, they are not necessarily important to what we are doing here.

SO, let's jump into each one of these individually.

THE TEMPORAL LOBES are located roughly above and behind your ears (which makes sense since this is where auditory processing happens), and they are responsible for auditory cues and a primary manager for locating and storing memories. According to Blake Flourney over at Sciencing, "The temporal lobes are located at the sides of the brain and can be considered the "middle" region of each brain hemisphere. As a whole, the temporal lobe is the part of your brain in charge of memory storage, the process of hearing sounds, visual recognition of faces and objects, and the use of language. Though this seems like an incredible number of functions for one small part of the brain to command, the temporal lobes are actually more complex than they look; they contain a number of specialized substructures, including the Amygdala and auditory cortex, that perform a variety of high-level functions. At the same time, the temporal lobes aren't the only parts of the brain used in many of these mental processes – the frontal and parietal lobes make sense of processed sounds, for example, and the hippocampus creates the memories that the temporal lobe then stores and recalls." (4-1)

THE HIPPOCAMPI ARE SUPER INVOLVED in memory and learning and can be highly affected by psychological and neurological disorders, such as depression or anxiety; they also play a role in negative behaviors. "Hippocampus is vital for learning, memory, and spatial navigation. Connections between the hippocampus and neocortex are important for awareness of conscious knowledge. [28] An intricate balance is maintained during encoding of memories in hippocampus and retrieval of experiences from the frontal lobe." (4-2). Now I know you're thinking—"This doesn't sound too bad." Let's see what they say about depression and the destruction of the hippocampi. "Ever since the biological basis of depression is getting unfolded, evidence is accumulating that prolonged depression can cause volume loss of hippocampus. Moreover, the duration of depression has been correlated with the severity of hippocampal atrophy. Evidence suggests that atrophy thus produced may be permanent and persist long even though depression has undergone remission. It has been hypothesized that it could be a consequence of affective disturbance seen in depression. It is believed that this could result from prolonged stress due to depression." (4-3)

THE AMYGDALA IS LOCATED deep in the temporal lobe and is shaped like an almond. It serves many purposes and connects deeply with fear and pleasure. The amygdala plays a *huge* role in processing emotions. Now one would assume that with it playing a huge role in processing emotions, we would want to keep it healthy; however, a variety of factors can also harm the amygdala. Everything from anxiety and depression to phobias can damage the amygdala's functions. Let's face it, with our current programming and superhighway bullshit, we are not getting very far from anxiety or depression. Dr. Anthony Wright states, "Amygdala is the integrative center for emotions, emotional behavior, and motivation. If the brain is turned upside down, the end of the structure continuous with the hippocampus is called the uncus. If you peel away uncus, you will expose the amygdala, which abuts the anterior of the hippocampus. Just like with the hippocampus, major pathways communicate bidirectionally and contain both efferent and afferent fibers." (4-4)

THE ENTORHINAL CORTEX is like the program that makes the computer work. It is the main interface that talks to both the hippocampi and the neocortex; it also acts as a navigation tool, a great teller of time, and a memory retriever. The entorhinal cortex's connection to the hippocampi is super important in the memory field. When I say super important, I mean it. The main purpose of this connection is memory formation, memory consolidation, and memory optimization while we sleep. The entorhinal cortex is also responsible for the recognition of the input signals to basically "identify" if we have a memory of this situation/event/or circumstance to go off of for our current event.

WE HAVE those main parts down; how do we break them down to mean anything to us, and how do they work together in shaping our reality?

EVERYTHING REALLY WORKS in concert together to shape how we perceive reality.

WHEN YOU RECEIVE INFORMATION, your brain instantaneously tries to find anything in its files that is similar or the same as the current situation you are in.

IF THE BRAIN finds any similar information, it will instantly "attach" this new event to the previous ones. It won't make a new "file"; it will simply file this new event with the others like it.

So, like a computer, if you already have a folder on your desktop for family pictures, you're probably not going to make a new folder for new family pictures. You'll likely make a subfolder for the current family photos within the first folder. The same can be said for these attached memories.

We don't go around all willy-nilly, making tons of folders when events or situations are similar; we simply throw the current event in with the similar events or make a subfolder if it's "kinda" the same.

USING the information we just learned about the super important parts of the brain, we can see that how we are feeling may, in fact, affect the way we perceive incoming memory and store it. Let me explain.

YOUR INCOMING MEMORY is skewed when you are sad, angry, or even tired. The same can be said when you're attempting to retrieve the memory. If you're in a happy mood when recalling negative memories, you're more likely to recall them being less unhappy than they actually were.

AN EXAMPLE of this would be, do you remember any negative sounds from your wedding day? Maybe a dog barking, an airplane overhead?

No.

That's because your brain selectively edited them out to focus on the happy.

WE ARE BEING TRIGGERED ALL the time, every day. If we touch, smell, taste, hear, or see something, and *also* certain colors, patterns, shapes, feelings, sounds, et al can be triggers. It can be vast or super specific. So, for example, you could be triggered by every beach or you could be triggered by a specific boardwalk, on a specific beach, during specific weather conditions.

. . .

YOUR NERVOUS SYSTEM is being triggered all the time, and it floods your brain with every activity, touch, smell, sound, taste, and sight it can associate with that trigger. This is a constant thing. There is no "take time off on Friday because we are going out." You are receiving information and thereby triggers all day long, and your brain does what it does and makes the relevant associations.

THIS LEADS us to the reasoning that if we are always inundated with "trigger" memories (IE, your brain's "truth" memories...because you know trauma), your brain doesn't really have "downtime." It is *always* in this "trigger" memory trauma mode. Do you want to guess what constantly living in "trigger" trauma mode does? Anxiety, depression, control issues, anger issues, and just all the yucky stuff you don't really like or want to think about.

SO, it's super important to do this work.

NEXT, we have false memories...mwahahahahaha.(I feel like some evil scientist when I say that. Seriously. Mainly because it seems like the work of science fiction.)

FALSE MEMORIES *ARE* A THING.

OUR MEMORY IS nothing like a video camera or a recording of an event that would provide us with an accurate retelling of the event. Memory is more like recalling certain components of the event, like the main idea or triggers. Everything else, the brain kind of just "fills in" based on your previous experience with something like the event in question.

A GOOD WAY TO understand this in a realistic way is to imagine your memory like a search engine's predictive search bar. You don't have to enter your whole statement. In fact, after you enter the first word, the predictive search bar starts populating all the possibilities it could be.

SALVADOR DALI FAMOUSLY SAID, "The difference between false memories and true ones is the same as for jewels: it is always the false ones that look the most real, the most brilliant."

NOT ONLY CAN our memories be influenced by our mood (or the mood of the filter we are currently using), but *completely fake memories can be in your noodle too!*

I KNOW, right?

SO MANY STUDIES have been done about implanting totally false memories and how the average participant recalled these fake memories.

For instance, Ira Hyman, Troy H. Husband, and F. James Billing of Western Washington University asked college students to recall childhood experiences that had been recounted by their parents. The researchers told the students that the study was about how people remember shared experiences differently. Hyman found that students fully or partially recalled 84 percent of the true events in the first and 88 percent in the second interviews. None of the participants recalled the false event during the first interview, but 20 percent said they remembered something about the false event in the second interview. (4-5)

WHAT'S interesting to note about this particular study (if you're so inclined to go look at it) is that some of the participants started to actually recall vivid details about the false memories.

THERE ARE numerous cases of patients suing their psychologist or psychiatrist and winning for false implanted memories. (If you want to go down the rabbit hole on that, a quick google search will do ya, I promise.)

SO, how susceptible are we to false memories?

EH. It's honestly tough to say. Really. The odds are pretty likely you're walking around with a few false memories. It could be something as innocent as, "remember that time we did that crazy thing?" And you have *no idea* what Jim is talking about, but you also don't want to be left out, so you go "oh, yeah..." and listen intently as Jim fills in the details for you. This memory is likely to be stored in your brain now.

HOW DOES this affect what we are doing?

. . .

WELL, unless you're dealing with nasty false memories, this process is unlikely to bother or eliminate those memories. Which some researchers say is a good thing.

Some researchers actually reiterate what I will tell you right now.

FALSE MEMORIES CAN BE USED for *good*, to alter memories of a negative nature into a more positive nature and therefore alter your future actions.

SIT AND THINK FOR A SECOND. If you go in and change the negative memories to positive memories (implanting yourself with false memories) and also tell others this new story, how will your future actions then be changed due to this new memory?

I WANT to be very clear here that I am in no way advocating for you to cover up the issue with false memories. The recourse of this is unknown, and quite frankly, I would be afraid to see what that would do. I am bringing the false memories into your sphere, though, so you can look at it as an option. I have not done extensive research on this subject, so I cannot be a guidepost here.

THIS LEADS us right back to the law of attraction. (I know I said I wouldn't, but this was literally *right there*). If your brain can do this with false memories, holding tightly onto the knot ball of shit, imagine what it can do with a slightly less tight grip on your knot ball. I mean, super cool, right?

· · ·

So, when we are looking at what our brain says is "reality," it may not be as real as we think it is. We have so many factors vying for control in our brains. The brain has its initial "truth" it's fervently holding onto, and we have all these "filters" we have working with or against the "truth" narratives, society telling us different things, our family telling us different things, and then still false memories telling us other things. It's a hot freaking mess in there sometimes, no joke.

BUT WE CAN MAKE it less of a hot mess.

CHANGING THE "TRUTH" THE
BRAIN THINKS WITH MUSIC

*I*n the past, I have received a lot of questions about this "truth," brain, music connection. And I will be the first to say it is quite confusing, to say the least. I tried my very best to get all the information here in an easily readable form, but after the first round of edits, I felt compelled to clarify this section. So, now it gets its own awesome chapter which will give you more of a common man breakdown of how it works.

WE'VE ESTABLISHED that the brain is a big fat liar and that it is easily influenced. Perhaps too easily. There is tons of evidence about "false memories" and how they can be implanted by others into your life. We also have evidence about how our memories are often skewed due to a variety of circumstances. September 11, 2001 is a prime example of skewed memories.

· · ·

ACCORDING TO DR. WILLIAM HIRST, "New research revolving around Americans' memories about 9/11 found that 40 percent of the time, their stories about that day changed as years passed.

Human memory is not like a computer. Human memory is extremely fallible." (5-1)

People can vividly remember watching the towers fall from their school, across the river...which isn't really possible. So, what the brain did was take the traumatic, life-changing event of September 11 that we actually experienced and melded it with what we saw and heard from others.

"Brown and Kulik (1977) suggested the term *flashbulb memory* for the "circumstances in which one first learned of a very surprising and consequential (or emotionally arousing) event," for example, hearing the news that President John Kennedy had been shot." (5-2) This would also apply to an event like September 11th. These "flashbulb" events are significant. They are not run of the mill, everyday, I stubbed my toe events. They are likely world-changing events that tilt the axis of the world, so to speak. When a lot of media coverage is given to one event, and when everyone we know is talking about an event, we want to feel included, and we also begin to add our stories to the event. However, we often take what we hear or see in the media and from our friends and family and "meld" that with what we actually felt, saw, or witnessed.

This isn't to say that all of what we remember is a lie but more that the brain and our memories are fallible. We can remember things differently than they really happened, and oftentimes, external influences and already placed memories play a role in these different memories.

So, those memories that you have of an event or situation may not be exactly what happened; in fact, you may have input previous memories or experiences that your brain fills in if there are gaps in the event or if the event is like one you've previously experienced.

Let me explain. When we think of past events, even traumatic ones, the memory clouds it with details that have "layered" memories because those have more significance (if you're questioning this, go re-read about the knot ball), and most of the time, those layer memories are the ones that fit the "pre-fit" dialogue that the brain has written. Whew! How confusing does that sound?

Let me give you an example from my past.

My first marriage was turbulent at best. There were good times, as there are always "highs" in those types of relationships, and then there were the "lows," which I found myself dwelling on when we were there in the low. But more than that, I carried those lows with me. I never forgot them or let them go. As the highs and lows ebbed and flowed like the tides, I would wait patiently because I knew it would not be too long before the other shoe dropped and we plummeted back to the lows, and I was once again vulnerable. I tried to guard myself as best as I could, shielding myself from any pain that I knew would come. (sidebar, this is not a "woe is me" point. I wouldn't change anything in my life; it all led me to where I am supposed to be, even in these bad, ugly times.) Honestly, I wore them (the pain, fear, anger) like a badge. Wrapping that unhappiness with me and carrying it with me everywhere I went. I would be angry and would carry that sadness with me even if I was wearing a "happy" face, even if I had mastered the mask that everyone saw because that's what I wanted them to see. That is probably the comment I got the most—"Why are you getting divorced? You seem so happy." I made it my "job" to be happy or at least make people think I was happy. So, all the events that happened that were "happy," I clouded with my "filters/layers" of past events. I was waiting for the other shoe to drop; I was not truly happy, just fake happy, under it all. The filters still clouded over the new incoming memories, making my unhappiness even more apparent to me.

I give you this background, these details, so that when I tell you my ex-husband and I are friends now (I mean, the man stays at my home when he's in town—we are legitimate friends), you'll know I had to look at the reality of the situation instead of the clouded past that often interferes with memories. If I looked at the situation from the "memory" perspective, my marriage sucked; it was a long-term abusive relationship that held me as the victim. That's what the memory plays. None of the good memories, none of the positive points, nothing but the negative. And also to let you know that the memory is also a big fat liar.

How so, you may ask?

Because remember when we talked about how the brain finds things in situations that fit the narrative that it has chosen as your truth? It doesn't matter that you got laid off because the company closed; your brain sees it as "I got laid off because I'm not good enough." So, when we think about things like divorce, there really isn't a positive "image" with it. Divorce is seen as a failure (even if it was the right thing to do). It's not necessarily taboo, but it doesn't leave a glowing impression either. So, the mind will feed this already perceived negative event (even if it was the right thing to do) into whatever your playing narrative is.

For me, it was like this...

Even though I know divorce was the right thing to do for myself, my ex-husband, and our children, my brain told me that I couldn't make marriage work because I wasn't good enough. I wasn't the best wife, I didn't try enough, and I wasn't "enough" of whatever was needed. It was my fault.

See how screwed up that is? Eff you, brain!

So, even societal events or pressures play this role in how

you react to an event and therefore store the memory. You don't even have to know someone who is divorced or went through a

"nasty" divorce; you have heard about it somewhere from someone, I promise. No matter how you reason with yourself that the divorce is a good thing for everyone involved, you will still likely feel like a failure, and you will likely second guess yourself the entire way.

And these "truths," you likely don't know. You may really only realize the emotions they elicit at this point. "I feel like such a failure." "I can't do anything right." "Why does no one like me?" And on and on that goes.

It really is your inner running monologue (unless you're one of those weirdos who don't have an inner monologue); that is a pretty good gauge of your "truth."

Is your inner monologue mostly positive, or is it more negative? How often do you chastise yourself daily? How often do you praise yourself daily? What is your inner monologue saying when you complete a task? What about when you don't complete a task? There are so many ways to self-check and gauge what you're saying to yourself. And this has been going on since before you can remember, that "truth" the brain has held onto and built over the years...it has been nurturing and building this truth for a lifetime.

Music has also been there for your lifetime (and beyond), quietly playing in the background of your life. Music is either playing in our heads or in reality for every success and failure, for every love-filled moment and fight.

So, sometimes, we don't need physical music playing for us to implement it into a memory. That's right! We can simply think of a song that evokes a similar emotional pattern as if we were truly experiencing it.

So, for example, we can win something *big*, something we have been working toward and striving for, then someone can make an off-handed comment about how this is a "champion" moment, and you could bring in *We Are The Champions* by Queen or you could honestly start playing it on your own, with no prompting.

Think for one second about how many times you have a song "stuck" in your head? How many times do you just start humming or singing a song? How often do you think or say, "I want to listen to Led Zeppelin today?"

I'm going to bet once you stop and take stock of this, it's probably a lot higher than you thought.

You are probably like me and think, "No way, I don't do that." Start keeping track, and you'll likely go, "OK, maybe I do that."

Don't worry. I did the same thing.

Music is just another connector to our world; it's probably one of the best connectors to our world because we don't have to say anything. We don't have to sing along if we don't want to, we don't have to talk, but we do *feel* it. We use our emotions to connect to the music and therefore to our world.

You can easily change or reaffirm your emotional mood with what you're listening to. Now, tastes in music vary, and you may not like what I do, but the truth is music *does* affect your emotional state and how you perceive the world.

THE BRAIN ~ EYE ~ SOUND TRICK THAT MAKES YOUR REALITY NOT SO REAL

*I*n this chapter, we are going to dive deep to explain the *why* (just like our EMDR chapter where we dove deep to explain it all) and how to mostly fix it because let's face it, the brain is quite easily the most complicated thing on the entire planet.

WE'VE all heard of someone moving across the country and getting stranded somewhere due to some emergency. Then they are stuck in BFE, either maxing credit cards or emptying savings to fix the "emergency," so they can get where they need to. Some of us may recall that person truly got "stuck" there, not having the funds or access to funds to fix the situation, so they just started a new life in BFE.

BUT WHO WAS THIS?

Can anyone remember?

Surely, if we've all heard this, it has to be true, right? It's like common knowledge or something.

. . .

WRONG.

There are maybe like two whole people that this scenario would apply to. But we were all nodding our heads in agreement to this story like it was true and something to take caution of.

LET me re-write that narrative for you so that you know an actual person this happened to.

I have moved across the country twice and across an ocean once, and not a thing happened that wasn't fixable.

Seriously.

MY MOST RECENT move was with four kids, two cars, one dad, one UHaul towing another car, two dogs, and four cats.

We moved the day after Christmas.

Through rain and snow across 3/4ths of the United States.

And not one thing happened!

Like seriously.

The worst thing that happened was a grandpa/dad who did not want to stop because we had deadlines (insert eye roll from frustrated daughter), and instead of taking 3-4 days like we were going to, we left on the 26th and got there in the early morning hours of the 28th.

ANOTHER EXAMPLE.

A friend of mine is trying to find a home for herself and her family. She has moved across the country three times in the past two years (no joke). They have four kids, a bunch of dogs, two parents, and a partridge in a pear tree. They travel with their *big* SUV and a travel trailer/5th wheel type thing. I think they also drive a moving truck.

They *always* have something go wrong.

I mean, that truthfully.

This last time, their SUV broke down three different times.

Each time, they camped, got it fixed, and moved forward to their destination.

Not one thing happened to them that wasn't fixable.

Mom and Dad also had some pretty awesome attitudes throughout the whole thing.

So, now I've given you two examples of cross-country moves, with families and animals in tow, and not a darn thing happened. So, what's the deal? Why are we stuck in the narrative that *something* bad will happen?

Just because your brain plays you the narrative of "what if this happens, we know it's possible" does not make it true.

Not one little bit.

I bet you're still thinking of who you know who had those issues moving.

I bet you're still coming up empty-handed.

Likely because it is a work of Hollywood fiction, and your brain cannot distinguish between what is "real truth" and what is "imagined/entertainment truth."

I know it's weird, right. Well, not so much.

When your brain receives visual clues that "something is happening," it automatically sends signals to your memory centers to locate and retrieve similar information. This is so the brain can do a quick compare and contrast to see if this new information is worth saving or not.

So, what we perceive as a real threat when coming up on decisions like this may be nothing more than Hollywood magic that our brain filtered in where it had no business being. Then you worry it to death and base your decision to stay in fear, based on a situation that has no relevance to you.

So, let me give you an example, the movie *Twister*. If you've seen the movie, you likely remember the end scene where they survive the twister by chaining themselves to a pipe and "riding the storm." When it saw that, maybe (most likely), your brain filed that under "Holy shit, we are going to die but try this first." And if you were ever in the unlikely situation that you had to chain yourself to an underground pipe to survive, you'd remember this working. It doesn't mean it will work in real life; in fact, it likely will never work in real life. I mean, the various things that could happen while chained are greater than just getting swept up by a tornado. But because our brains saw this situation as plausible and a survival scenario, it likely did save this information. Even if you've never been in a twister and your chance of being in one is slim to none. It is a plausible situation for the brain, so the data was saved.

NOW YOU'RE PROBABLY WONDERING what this has to do with what we are doing with the brain and music and let me tell you, it's actually quite ingenious. Just like the brain stores your memories with additional stimuli (music, sights, smells, textile, etc.), the brain also stores these imagined truths with the additional stimuli, but because there were no additional stimuli (you were not actually in the situation to receive stimuli), the brain filled in the blanks.

That's right, your good ol' brain, which is always trying to make things easier for you and protect you, does it again by filling in the blanks of things it does not know entirely but are similar to something it does know.

ACCORDING to Allison Sekuler at the University of Toronto, "What many people don't realize is that the objects we see are not necessarily the same as the information that reaches our eyes, so the brain needs to fill in those gaps of missing information."

Furthermore, directly from their research...

"THE GROUP OF RESEARCHERS, led by Ph.D. students Jason Gold and Richard Murray, asked people to describe various types of shapes presented on different backgrounds made up of visual "noise"—gray, black, and white pixels similar to the snow on a de-tuned television. The square shapes were either real, illusory, blocked or fragmented.

BECAUSE THE OBJECTS were difficult to see, sometimes they appeared fat or thin, depending on the background noise. (The sides of fat objects bend outward while the sides of thin objects bend inward.) By averaging the luminance of the visual noises that led to fat or thin responses, the researchers determined which parts of the stimulus were important for these judgments.

. . .

NOT SURPRISINGLY, the researchers said, when there really were contours in the shape that made it thin or fat, people used information around the location of these defining lines in making the shape discrimination. "Amazingly, however, we found that people used information from exactly the same locations even when the contours in those locations were hidden or missing altogether. In other words, people relied on contours that were not really there, but that had been constructed by their brains," says Gold, whose thesis is looking at the mechanisms underlying visual perception.

"IF YOU DIDN'T HAVE the brain filling in all of this missing information, every time you looked at an object from a slightly different view, it would be a different object, and that would be very confusing and difficult to cope with," says Patrick Bennett, associate professor of psychology at U of T and the study's other senior author. "This filling in gives some consistency and continuity to the world." (7-2)

So, there you have it...the brain makes up s#!t and passes it off as truth to you if it looks kinda like that other thing.

So, you know the friend who had issues moving that no one can really remember who it was? I have it for you.

Does anyone remember the movie *Doc Hollywood* starring Michael J. Fox?

He was moving...

Broke down...

He was stuck in some tiny town that happened to need a doctor...

He ended up staying there and starting a new life...

. . .

THAT'S YOUR FRIEND.

YOUR BRAIN TOOK this Hollywood fiction work and said, "Yep, this is a possibility; let me file that for later."

AND NOW, every time you say, "Maybe I should see what life is like in this state or country," your brain pulls this Michael J. Fox scenario out (or worse if we are thinking of moving out of the country...I mean, just turn on the news for five seconds to hear some horror story about somewhere else in the world) and removes the characters *and* that it's a movie and says, "No, no we can't! See what can happen?"

THE BRAIN not only does this with moving but, of course, not. When we are dealing with more intimate things, say leaving an abusive relationship, the brain pulls every news story it's ever heard about leaving abuse going horribly wrong. This, coupled with your diminished self-image from the abuse, is why you stay.

ALL THOSE UNDER-EMPLOYED and unemployed people you hear about are the reason you stay in a job you loathe. (Well, part of the reason, but honestly, that topic of how poorly this country is run, and no, I don't just mean the president, in and of itself, is a whole other book)

. . .

IT'S the reason you're afraid to find what truly makes you happy. Because people who are happy are like freaks and something *always* goes wrong for them. Because you know you've heard forever that no one really likes their job or how you should just "take the job" because of bills and all.

THERE IS ALWAYS some horror story that the brain has witnessed somewhere that it will literally replay for you to keep you right in the spot you are.

FEAR IS an agent of destruction and one of the most powerful emotions. It is the brain's easiest way to deter you from anything it feels would be harmful to you, so it can keep you safe.

SURPRISINGLY, or perhaps not so surprisingly, now that you've read this book so far, we make a lot of emotional connections to memories in our brain via music, and these musical memories also play a big part in our fear triggers and keeping up the status quo.

LET ME EXPLAIN.

WE WILL TAKE something we are all familiar with, the tell-tale notes of a suspense or horror scene in a movie.

NONE of us have ever actually heard this soundtrack playing in the background of our life when bad things happen.

. . .

BUT WHAT HAPPENS when we hear the oh-so-familiar notes start to play?

WE INSTANTLY FEEL FEAR.

THE TINGLING in our stomach starts as we anticipate something bad happening.

WE HAVE BEEN TRAINED, through media influence and their understanding of our brain and how it works, that it is a suspenseful or fearful situation when we hear this specific type of music.

EVEN THOUGH WE have no actual memory or personal knowledge to base this on, our brain takes the information from the movie (both the visual and audial cues) and puts it in the "shit that won't ever happen, but it just may, so I am going to save this to scare the shit out of you category" for 500, Alex!

So, now we hear the notes, the rustle in the trees at night, or any number of audial cues the brain has stored, and bam, you have fear running like ice in your veins.

THE SAME CAN ALSO BE SAID about non-Hollywood audial cues.

. . .

THAT TIME you got into a really bad car accident, and Blues Traveler was playing, and now you can't stand them and don't know why?

MAYBE YOU WALKED down the aisle to a non-traditional wedding song and then got divorced, and now the song makes you physically ill.

THERE ARE a million examples I can give you in relation to music playing a role in your brain filling in the pieces or just flat out making things up; however, by now, I hope you get the point.

So, besides the brain making things up and fear ruling the roost, what else is keeping you in the same spot, reliving the same mistakes, doing the same things?

SIMPLY PUT, you have not unraveled your knot ball of shit. You will keep reliving the same patterns regardless of whether you tell the brain that it was just a movie and you know no one in real life who was stuck in the middle of nowhere. Because you're still living on the same super-highway of crap that you've been living on.

THE STEPS ARE before you to undo the superhighway that has kept you in the same spot. It's up to you to make the conscious choice to want something more, better, and alive.

WHAT WE'VE LEARNED IN A NUTSHELL

*T*his chapter is for those who don't have a lot of time, want the Cliff notes version, or just want a general review of what we have learned.

And we've learned a lot. Like, seriously, a lot.

So, just like right before our big test...let's review!

We have learned that *before* birth, our brain starts making connections to music, emotions, and feelings.

We have learned that these connections make "truths" that form our belief patterns for life.

We've learned that these belief patterns or "truths" run on a superhighway.

We've learned that unless we make a conscious effort to make a new highway, we will continue to run on the old pattern of the superhighway.

This superhighway is so big, wide, and deep that it takes serious effort on our parts to get to the center of our knot ball of shit.

We have learned that unless we remove and replace this knot ball of shit, we will continue on the same pattern forever ...(((*forever*)))

We have learned our brains are *big, fat liars!* Seriously.

Our brain cannot tell the difference between a fact that happened to us and is a real possible threat and what is Hollywood fiction.

As such, we must be super vigilant about what the brain tells us as "fact."

We have learned that we can change the way the brain thinks and, by proxy, what our truth is.

The truth is that everything is changeable, including the way our brain thinks and what it believes is truth. The brain won't like it, the brain won't want you to try to change how it works, and the brain will try to throw some very real, fear-laden things at you in an attempt to get you to stop.

But…

We've learned that fear is the number one obstacle that prevents us from changing.

And we learned that fear is the brain's first and last attempt to get you to stop what it doesn't want you to do.

It will try any and every fear trick in the book with you to get you to stop changing things.

But we should not listen to it.

We move past the fear.

We move beyond fear.

Because we know better than that.

We know that the brain sees what it wants to and does what it thinks is best even though it may not actually be.

We are designed for better than that.

We are here for better than that.

We *are* better than that.

Start claiming that, right now!

We will start focusing on the core memories and start with the first song you wrote down as it is likely the most significant to you as it was the first to pop into your memory. So, in order to prepare for the exercises in the next chapter, get comfortable, grab your handy dandy notebook (you need a notebook for the exercises, I promise!), and let's get to work.

HOW TO FIND THE CENTER OF YOUR KNOT BALL OF SHIT...BECAUSE YOU NEED TO

** *W* ARNING**
This may be an ugly chapter for you. You may cry hot, fat, ugly tears that turn into a straight-up ugly cry with the snot running down your face and you not giving one hot damn. But it's OK. You need this. The sooner you face the center of your knot ball of shit, the sooner you can start to heal the hurt, and that, my friends, is the end goal...healing.

So, this is an activity chapter...woohoo! Get a pad of paper or, better yet, a composition notebook denoted specifically for this (you'll need it), and a pen/pencil/quill and ink, whatever you feel comfortable writing with. Now before you start asking questions, yes, it needs to be handwritten. The short and sweet explanation for this is because the brain attaches emotional significance and importance to things you write out versus when you write on a keyboard or talk to text. It has something to do with the wiring from your ancestors from caveman days that has been encoded into your DNA, important stuff. They wrote (or drew), and this tradition has carried through the centuries. So, for the love of everything, get some damned paper and write.

FIRST THINGS FIRST...DATE this. The way to truly measure progress is to look back and see how far we've come, which is exactly what we are doing here by dating this. We can look back months from now and see if we still hold emotional significance to certain things we have written.

NEXT, let's write down all the negative events we can remember from childhood. Now, don't go searching the depths of your mind to find these; most will stick out like a sore thumb. You know those events we replay in the wee hours of the night, those events that replay over and over with what we "should have" done or said—start with these because they don't hang around your brain for no reason nagging you. They are there for clues...ah ha, Sherlock, you've found your first one. Don't worry about finding all the negative events at one time; once you open the flood-gates, you will automatically start remembering more, but for now, let's start with what you automatically remember with little to no effort. Make a list in your composition note-book however you feel is best. You can make your list chronologically, most hurtful, by periods of your life, what-ever makes the most sense to you. List everything you can remember and then move on to the next stage, locating the core beliefs behind the majority of your hurtful memories.

It's important to note here that you don't want to hang around "looking" for stuff. Believe me when I say that these things will start coming to you automatically. Do not sit there and analyze what you have written down; just acknowledge it and move on. Do not sit there and question why you automatically wrote something down; your brain knows where it needs to start, so it will take you right where it needs to or wants to go.

NOW THAT YOU have a list of some negative memories, you may have three, or you may have 13. Literally, there is no right or wrong answer here. You can start the next process if you have something written on that paper.

NOW LET'S take a look at some common negative core beliefs.

These are what most people identify with in some way or another. Right now, we are looking for the "big, bad, and ugly" ones. Believe me when I say you will recognize them once you read them and when you read one that you "feel," write it down and move on to the next. After you have identified all your "big, bad, and ugly" core beliefs, you can then start attaching events or memories that you have to each core belief to see if it fits.

For example, we will fall back onto our chapter one example of "they don't want me." If you "feel" a resonance with "not good enough, I have no value, I am worthless," then we start attaching the job we didn't get, the girl who left us, and so on...does this "fit" with what this means to us? If it does, then huzzah!. You have located part, if not all, of the center of your knot ball of shit, and you can begin to work to repair the damage. Suppose it does not apply to the majority of the situations in your life that are damaging. In that case, this belief pattern may have been adopted along the way and added additional layers to your knot ball, but sadly, it is not the center. You'll still have to work to remove this particular belief pattern as you have adopted this as truth at some point in your life, but it's not the mega, superhighway truth. You can also read through the list and examples and then write the ones that "fit" next to each hurtful memory. Example: I didn't get the job promotion that I wanted/deserved, so "I am not good enough, I am powerless" would fit there, so write that next to the unreceived promotion and then move on down the list. Do not dwell on any one of these for too long. You are just analyzing this at the moment; you're not going in-depth as to why didn't you do X, Y, or Z when the boss said there is no one more deserving of this promotion than Sally when you knew damned well you did all of Sally's work and you should have said something then. No, stop. Do not go down this rabbit hole. Just observe the feelings that come up and record them with the hurtful memory or in groups of memories.

So, let's go through this shit list of common negative core beliefs, and be sure to read through each supporting belief *and* their typical belief issues. If any of that resonates within you anywhere, note it and come back to find the emotion you feel. Don't try to do it all at once. You can become easily overwhelmed with this process. It is totally normal to read back on this in a day, week, or month and find that you now have more memories or emotions than you previously had for a certain belief pattern. If you can only note the emotion (unfair, sad, angry, whatever) and not a specific event (I didn't get the job promotion), that is OK. Note it (as this is an experience you are feeling, and we need to validate it), and move on. Don't stress yourself trying to find a situation, life event, or memory that fits it, as your brain may have hidden it from itself and you, and all you are left with is this "belief" or feeling/emotion. As we progress through this, more will become clear to you, so if you can't "put your finger" on the memory or situation but the belief resonates with you, note it, move on, and revisit in a few days.

COMMON NEGATIVE CORE BELIEFS:

CORE BELIEF ~ I am worthless.
  Supporting beliefs ~ I have no value ~ I am not good enough ~ I have nothing to offer anyone ~ I am not interesting enough ~ I am not smart enough ~ I am unimportant ~ I am nobody.
  Typical belief issues ~ Self-worth/self-esteem ~ receiving gifts ~ receiving compliments.

CORE BELIEF ~ I am powerless
  Supporting beliefs ~ I am unsuccessful ~ I am inferior ~ I am unworthy ~ I can't change ~ I will fail ~ I am disposable ~ I am not good at anything.
  Typical belief issues ~ achievement ~ standards ~ success ~ goals ~ results ~ organization ~ self-empowerment ~ ability to make changes.

CORE BELIEF ~ I am wrong/unsure
  Supporting beliefs ~ I am always wrong ~ I am not understood ~ I cannot understand ~ I can't trust people ~ I am not trustworthy ~ I am mistaken ~ it isn't fair.
  Typical belief issues ~ right and wrong ~ justice ~ openness ~ honesty ~ trust ~ trustworthiness ~ understanding.

. . .

CORE BELIEF ~ I am defective/not right

Supporting beliefs ~ It's my fault ~ I am guilty ~ I am not whole/perfect ~ I am bad ~ I am ugly ~ I am fat ~ I can't be me ~ I am useless ~ I am a failure ~ I will fail ~ I am a loser ~ I will lose ~ I don't deserve anything ~ I am stupid ~ I am unattractive ~ There's something wrong with me.

Typical belief issues ~ emotional age ~ growth ~ balance between giving and receiving.

CORE BELIEF ~ I am nothing/I don't exist

Supporting beliefs ~ I am worthless ~ I am invisible ~ I am nothing ~ I am nobody ~ I am not enough ~ I am insignificant ~ I will never be recognized.

Typical belief issues ~ being your authentic self ~ my knowledge ~ my experience ~ who I am is not what I do ~ individuality.

CORE BELIEF ~ I am unlovable/unwanted

Supporting beliefs ~ I am not lovable ~ I am always left out ~ I am alone ~ I don't matter ~ I am not wanted ~ I am not special ~ I am unimportant ~ I don't fit in anywhere.

Typical belief issues ~ nobody loves me ~ nobody wants me ~ unconditional love ~ self-care ~ self-love ~ accepting care ~ accepting help ~ accepting love.

ALTHOUGH THERE ARE QUITE a few other "minor" categories, such as "I have lost my spirit" and "I am not real," these six are the primary ones the majority of people identify and struggle with. Let's go through some examples for each so that we can "put a face to it," so to speak. I find that sometimes it is easier to "jog" the brain's memory and put our finger on our memories/events if we have examples to compare.

CORE BELIEF ~ I am worthless

EXAMPLE ~ We are invited to our spouse's work function. We don't want to go but at the same time know this is important to our spouse's career. We don't know anyone other than our spouse and cannot imagine what they would want to talk to us about, let alone begin to fathom how we are going to start a conversation with a person. We generally stay glued to our spouse's side, don't say much, and maybe even outwardly complain to our spouse that we have nothing in common with these people. We cannot imagine why anyone would want to talk to us anyway, as we certainly are not as important as everyone in this room; they are all so impressive. If we manage to initiate a conversation with someone, we instantly "tally" ourselves to the other person. Making mental notes about areas in which they are better than us, marveling at their amazingness, and mentally berating ourselves for not being good enough or making a list of things we need to change to be better. Our spouse senses our discomfort and typically cuts the evening short because we are being our typical wallflower self. Our spouse may become angry that we made them look bad, and we berate ourselves further that we cannot be more/better/smarter to make our spouse happy.

CORE BELIEF ~ I am powerless

. . .

EXAMPLE ~ You work in middle management. You give your
time to the company in the hopes of having your efforts
recognized by the bosses for the coveted promotion that you
(and everyone else) know is available. You work hard and
often go above and beyond the scope of your job. Your boss
assigns you and another co-worker a project to work on
together; you have a feeling this is because you two are the
front runners. Right off the bat, you notice that your co-
worker is not putting forth the effort they should be, so you
begin to pick up the pace in your own work, anticipating
that you will be asked to finish the project. Feeling really
good about your position, you balance your regular work-
load and this special project until you are finished and
present your work. Your boss thanks you and then excuses
you. Later that week, your boss calls a meeting, and you are
ready; today is the day you will get the promotion you
worked hard for. Your boss begins to praise your hard-
working department, telling how some people have learned
how to work smarter, not harder, to get more accomplished,
and this shows as an exemplary material for the new promotion. Then your boss says your co-worker's name and not
yours. You feel defeated, like you're never going to be
successful no matter how hard you try. You are somehow
inferior to everyone else, and you will never achieve the
successes others seem to enjoy so easily.

CORE BELIEF ~ I am wrong/unsure

EXAMPLE ~ No matter what I say, people seem to take my
words wrong. I may as well be speaking in a different
language sometimes. I often get frustrated when people don't
"get" what I am saying. I also have the feeling that I frustrate

them as well when my meaning is not interpreted correctly. This pattern is nothing new; I have always been on the wrong side of the right or just too utterly confused about a situation. This often leads to people not trusting me and/or me not trusting other people because what they said, they didn't mean, and now they are doing something else. I often feel like a mistake and that the Universe is playing some cruel joke on me, like I was in the wrong place at the wrong time when they were handing out the "cool" lives.

CORE BELIEF ~ I am defective/not right

EXAMPLE ~ EVERYTHING I do is my fault. I can never do anything right or even be right. I will never be good enough, nor will I ever achieve anything of importance. My sisters are just perfect, and then there's me...fat, ugly, hopeless, loser me. People often tell me that I am awkward or crazy, and they are likely right. I never feel like I can "be me" with anyone, even those I truly love because if they see the real me, they would likely run away screaming. I tend to use gifts to show people how much I care, but they don't seem to care back, leaving me feeling rejected. I am just a damaged human who is broken beyond all repair, and I am doomed to fulfill the mentally and emotionally challenging days of life alone. In games of chance, I am always the loser, and I don't think I have ever won anything in my life. I will just continue to sit in the corner and not be myself because who would ever love or want a rejected loser like me?

CORE BELIEF ~ I am nothing/I don't exist

. . .

EXAMPLE ~ I feel like the invisible man floating through life most days. Everybody else gets the recognition they deserve, but me...nope. No one sees me or what I do. I often feel worthless because no one values or appreciates me or my work. They never see even the big things I do, let alone the small things I have accomplished. I never feel like I am good enough for the recognition. Why would I be? I have not been good enough my whole life. I have always held the backseat compared to my brother. He was perfect, and here I am, an insignificant nothing. Sometimes I try to be what others want me to be, but I feel fake and not true to myself. I don't think I will ever be visible or even someone's first choice. I make a good backup plan, but most times, people rarely get to their backup plans, so I will just stay invisible forever.

CORE BELIEF ~ I am unlovable/I am unwanted

EXAMPLE ~ I have never been special; I mean, what is there that is special about me? I am rather plain and ordinary. I generally don't fit in anywhere...not like that matters as I am typically left out of everything anyway. Mom and Dad are never on my side, and I am always the one who goes without or is left out. I am not that interesting, and when I have something important or interesting to say, no one pays attention to it anyway. I feel alone in this world most days. I am constantly seeking reassurance from my spouse/partner that they love me because, quite frankly, I cannot believe it because nobody loves me, not even my parents. I don't really matter in the grand scheme of things, and I am just a nobody on the sidelines who is as uninteresting and unimportant as the wallpaper I am standing in front of.

. . .

READING THROUGH THESE, I want you to pay special attention to what you're feeling, not what your brain "wants" you to hear but what is actually playing through your brain when you read these. There is sometimes a really big separation from what our brain wants us to feel and see and what we are actually feeling. So, take stock, inside, push past the initial "naw that isn't me," and really look at what your body is saying to you. For some of you, this may come easily. "Ah, yep. This has been me my whole life." But for some of you, your brain will still try to hide what is causing you pain. "No, I am special, I am important, I am fantastic." What we cannot ignore in situations like this is how we feel. You hear people talk about "gut feelings," and this is one of those situations where you need to pay attention to your "gut feelings." How do you feel when you read the words and the examples? Do you feel uneasy or scared? Is there a ring of truth some-where? A lot of people report feeling a heavy heart, an upset stomach, and shortness of breath. Pay attention to your physical symptoms, too; they can tell you the truth even when your brain is doing its darndest to keep you from finding the truth. If you experience physical symptoms, note them down along with any feelings that you may notice with the physical symptom. If you have no specific feeling with the physical symptom, that is OK; just note what you are feeling on any level and move on.

WRITE down any of the specific feelings/memories/and core beliefs that you can identify:

_____

_____

NOW THAT YOU have your feelings/memories/or core beliefs down, let's begin to link them to each other and life events.

*Remember, these first ones are in no way all of it. It's where your brain said, "OK, let's start here."

CAN you link a feeling to the time you didn't get that promotion? What about a core belief? Can you find some memories that link to a core belief? Once you identify the feelings, you can start tugging the memories, and once you start tugging at the memories, you can find the core belief to start working on.

AS AN ASIDE, it is OK and quite common to identify with more than one of these. Some people are lucky and only have one negative core belief they deal with, and others (like me) are not so lucky. We start with a core belief, and because we are so affected by this belief, we begin to add additional core beliefs. Now, these don't necessarily add new "cores," but it does add complexity to your knot ball of shit. Instead of just having one core belief and the layers associated with it, you have your core belief and layers for that, then an added negative belief, and now you add in layers of that. So, you may go a while with "I am unlovable," and you will have layer upon layer of that, and then you get the idea that "I am powerless," and you begin to add layers of this. One day, you will begin to feel unlovable/unloved again, and this cycle will repeat on and on. So it is OK to identify with one, two, or all of the core beliefs. There are no right or wrong answers here, and we are just trying to get you to recognize the feelings and hopefully attach them to core beliefs.

IN ORDER TO recognize one core belief from the other, since a few are fairly similar, it all comes down to feelings. For example, if you are toggling between "I am defective" and "I am nothing," you will note that they are similar, and sometimes those emotions are indistinguishable from each other. I want you to write both down (it is possible that you have both core belief patterns) but also pay attention to the feelings. Do you always feel wrong or like everything is your fault? These subtle differences will make a difference in the long run.

Do these subtle nuances make a difference in the grand scheme? Why yes, they do. If you begin working on "I am defective" because "I can't figure this out, so whatever, I am going with this one," and in reality, it's more like "I am nothing," are you really working to unravel your knot ball of shit? No, you're not.

If you are unsure, leave them both and walk away from it. You heard that right.

You may have to write down both and pay attention to how you are feeling for a few days to a week. Note down when things "go wrong" and how you're feeling. (If you have not noticed, feelings are a huge part of this, so start paying attention to them, like, now.)

ONCE YOU HAVE a core belief or five identified, then we can move forward to what to do with them. Let's go!

HOW CAN MUSIC RELATE TO MY KNOT BALL OF SHIT?

*S*o, hopefully, now you know what your knot ball of shit is (if you did your homework. You did your homework, right? It's super important, so go do your homework, please), and how to identify the layers and the center. But how do we work to get rid of it, and how in the heck does music play into this all?

Relax... I've got you, and I wasn't just going to leave you out in the cold.

Read on, Grasshopper.

Do you remember how we talked about how memories get stored differently when multiple layers of stimuli are added to the initial memory? Yes, great job remembering stuff. That, my friend, is fantastic because that is literally the reason and the way to not only figure out the feelings that may not be visible to you but also how to use it to "move" the memories to long-term storage or garbage. You know, whichever works best.

. . .

I KNOW I am likely talking way too fast.I'm sorry. I get kinda jazzed about this. So, we will quickly review to refresh your memory and then make those needed links that connect the dots.

WE ARE GOING to revert back to the example that has served us well since the beginning, "daddy doesn't want me." Perhaps your mother liked classic rock (well, current rock at the time, but that's neither here nor there), and your brain processed this vital information as fact just as Queen's frontman Freddie Mercury was belting out *We Are the Champions*. I mean, who can resist the velvety pipes of Freddie Mercury? Everybody sings along to that one. Except now that song is also stored with the memory of daddy not wanting you. Your three-year-old brain, after perhaps years of absenteeism from Dad, decided that at the moment Mercury lets out the first chorus,

"I've paid my dues
Time after time
I've done my sentence
But committed no crime
And bad mistakes
I've made a few
I've had my share of sand kicked in my face."

that it all makes sense. "Time after time," Dad didn't want me. "I've committed no crime," he just doesn't want me.

So, we have a feeling, "dad doesn't want me," and we add in a layer of stimuli, Mercury's velvet voice, and perhaps another layer of stimuli because Mom's preparing meatloaf or maybe you were snuggled up with your blanket for comfort and listening to Freddy's pipes. That is three different layers of stimuli added onto this one memory. How much easier/faster/better do you think this memory will "stick" since we have three sensory inputs?

AND NOW WE have a complex memory, layered with different sensory information that "triggers" us.

BECAUSE YOUR PARENTS loved classic (then current) rock, you listened to all the greats while building on the center of your knot ball and the subsequent layers that were added every time you affirmed either through perceived reality or actual reality that "daddy doesn't want me." You may have a deep love of classic rock that brings emotions to the surface that you cannot explain, or you could absolutely hate classic rock and, for some reason you cannot quite put your finger on, just don't really like any of it. You could also be in the middle of the road and like most classic rock but absolutely detest the pipes of Freddy Mercury.

NO MATTER YOUR feelings on the subject of classic rock, you have some sort of feeling or emotion tied to classic rock, and this is the heart of the matter. Music ties into our feelings and emotions. If you're married, I bet you can tell me the exact feeling you have when you hear your wedding song to this day, or if there was music playing during your first kiss, perhaps you can recall your first concert, and I am willing to put money on if I was standing right in front of you while you were telling me all the details, you would have a happier expression than you did two minutes ago. Speaking of details, I also know that those moments in time, when music flooded into and layered an additional layer of stimuli onto the memory, you can likely recall every minute detail of the event down to the smells.

BOTTOM LINE: When we have multiple layers of sensory input on a negative memory, feeling, or emotion, this memory/feeling/emotion intensifies greatly. This works for both positive and negative memories.

FIRST KISS ~ TOTALLY EASY, Tommy Murgich. He smelled of grass and what I've come to know is sweat.

First car crash ~ Bush Glycerine was playing on the radio, and the sound of breaking glass is one I will never forget.

The first time I felt proud ~ *Castle on the Cloud* was the song request, sung by yours truly.

The first time I was raped ~ Steve Miller Band *Fly Like an Eagle* was playing, and incense filled my nostrils.

MULTIPLE LAYERS of sensory input stick out like a sore thumb to our brain, and that's just what we do when we are layering sensory stimuli onto memories.

IT'S like reading a book and placing a bookmark at an important part you don't want to forget, then also placing a Post-it note there, then also bending the bottom corner because this is super important. We must never forget where this place is in the book. Odds are when we pick up this book we set down over a year ago, we will instantly flip to the bookmarked, Post-it noted, and bent corner page...not because we remember what was on the page but because we flagged it in such a way that draws our attention to it instantly.

BACK TO THE sensory memory input that we unwittingly take part in all the time.

YOU SEE, once you activate one sensory input into a memory, you are more likely to layer additional senses as well. It's similar to the brain finding faces on the moon. The brain tries very hard to put everything in groups or to link it to already known truths. This process is known as apophenia, and in the simplest terms, it is making connections between unrelated things, which coincidentally is what your brain does all day. The brain processes tons of information daily. I mean, the eye processes an image in about thirteen milliseconds, and the brain, in turn, processes roughly twenty million billion bits of information per second. So we should not find it very surprising that the brain attaches bits of information together to make its own process easier.

So, the feel of the fabric from your suit, the smell of your soon-to-be wife's flowers as she approached you, the feel of her glossed lips as you shared that precious first kiss as husband and wife...these other senses were activated when you heard *The Bride's March* and your heart signaled through rapid palpitations to the brain, that this was an important memory to be stored. And the brain does what it does and attaches every sensory stimulus to this moment for easier storage but also so that we can be reminded of the memory with the smell of flowers, the feel of glossed lips on ours, or upon hearing the first bars of the wedding march.

This memory can be brought up by not only actively searching for the memory but also through the music you remember, which is why this book is focused on music. Music can play such a vital role in not only *finding* the center of your knot ball of shit but also *unraveling* the knot ball.

NOW LET'S get down to the brass tacks. You have a pretty comprehensive list of your feelings and memories, and maybe you've even attached a few core beliefs...I am really hoping you've done your homework here because you'll need that information for this chapter. We are going to find the types of music you identify with the most in regards to core feelings, and from there, we can figure out feelings and, hopefully, your core belief systems.

There are six core emotions that spawn all other emotions, so it is fairly easy to tune into just the core six, although I will provide a chart with most of the corresponding emotional spawn so that if you're stuck, you can look through the other emotions and see if there is something that "clicks."

*THE BIG SIX ARE ANGER, **sadness, shame/ashamed, fear, love, and happiness.***

I WISH I was kidding when I wrote that out...seriously. But I'm not. There are four negative emotions in the top six and only two positive ones.

SIX PRIMARY EMOTIONS

INTENSITY/A PERIOD OF FEELING	LOVE	SAD	ANGRY	HAPPY	AFRAID	ASHAMED
HIGH						
MEDIUM						
LOW						

Now, if you know anything about emotions or have ever taken a Psychology 101 class, you are thinking I am pretty full of shit, saying there are only six primary emotions. You're probably saying something akin to, "What about Maslow's Hierarchy of Needs or Plutchik's Wheel of Emotions, Ms. Smarty Pants!" and you're right! Those are two very prominent and excellent examples of the complexity of emotions. However, at its core—the root of the emotion—it all boils down to just a few. There is new research using facial imaging that is even suggesting that all emotions boil down to four core starting points. So while Maslow and Plutchik are geniuses in their own right and certainly opened more doors than they could ever have imagined, we can link trailing emotions to just a few "core" emotions.

With four negative core emotions and only two positive core emotions, is it any freaking wonder we are so wrapped up with negativity and negative emotions? We are inundated with them on a daily basis. From every angle, it looks like we are forced to live in some state of negativity every second of our lives.

From a very young age, we begin to store things in our brain that we learn from our family and our environment. We store these things so we can later make connections to other things that our brains process. It may not all get stored as "fact." It could very well end up in the recycle bin, But we do store and catalog it "just in case" we run into something like it again. Once the brain recognizes a pattern with what we have already learned and new incoming information, it just adds the new information to the already linked, already learned knowledge. We learn that daddy making silly faces makes us happy, so we laugh, we learn that the mommy person gives us big hugs when we take our first steps, and that makes us happy, we learn that the brother person gets really angry when we draw him a picture on his book which makes us sad. As we get older, we can add environmental and societal factors to what our brain is processing, cataloging, and storing. The kids who made fun of you for "cheap shoes" made you feel ashamed of what you have and angry that you couldn't have nicer shoes. The magazine that featured the photoshopped perfectness of the latest new "it" girl, which is nowhere close to what you look like, made you feel ashamed of yourself and angry at yourself that you aren't "trying hard enough." And on I can go with examples into infinity, I promise.

So, when we are thinking in terms of our knot ball of shit and our musical choices, everything boils down to six, and those six have a "mood" in which you prefer to listen to a certain kind of music. Yeah, the balls are all falling into place now, aren't they?

. . .

So, the theory is that we see the more negative aspects of life, thus building upon our knot ball of shit, because we identify with more negative core feelings than positive ones. Think for a second about an infant. An infant knows very little about the environment in which it has just been born. It really only knows what it has heard for the last twenty or so weeks in its mother's womb. However, an infant's first emotional reaction is fear. Yeah, you heard that right. Infants are born afraid. Have you ever been holding an infant, and they flail their arms to the side to "catch" themselves from falling? Infants are born with a fear of falling. It is actually called the "startle reflex." We are born with a negative emotion already imprinted in our brains. No freaking wonder there are more negative core emotions than positive ones.

So, back to that really depressing figure of core emotions. We are going to use this to determine what core feelings you most relate to. This doesn't have to be perfect, and if you are not sure (just like in Chapter 2), just leave it alone for a little while and come back to it later. You are going to go through figures 3-1 and note each emotion you can attach to memory or just ones you feel without knowing why. Again, this may take a week or so, and that's OK!

WRITE ALL the core and sub-core emotions that you identify with here:

_____

_____

_____

NOW THAT WE HAVE MEMORIES, feelings, and emotions documented, it's time to start documenting our music preferences and dislikes. Everybody has their favorites when it comes to music. For some people, it is whole genres, and for others, it is specific songs. Either way is fine. Again, there are no right or wrong answers here. So, I want you to think— and this may take some time—but you're trying to find the emotional link to the inside of your brain, so I don't expect it to be easy.

TO HELP you in this process, I am going to gently guide you.

What music do you turn on without thinking when you're angry?

What do you listen to when you need a pick me up or motivation?

Do you have music you turn to when something great happens, and you want to celebrate?

What music speaks to your soul when you're sad and feel like giving up?

YOU GET THE IDEA. Ask yourself these or similar questions. You can leave the questions general as shown or get specific, "What do I want to listen to when Tom expects me to work full time and have dinner ready?" Or "What do I play when I go beast mode at the gym with the guys?" It's really about preference here, and the only thing that matters is getting the results, so if you are not getting the results with the more general questions, try some specific ones to jog you down a path.

LET ME GIVE YOU AN EXAMPLE. I am not a genre person. I am a song person. I attach significance to specific songs and not a whole genre, so my list of those I can remember looks like this. ***Note that my list is ever evolving as I listen to music and realize that this is something that affects me on an emotional level. This list is not stagnant but that is helpful for you. Once you learn to recognize the pattern of identifying negative emotions when they arise, you can "nip it in the bud" instead of letting it gain steam and build layers back onto your knot ball.

So back to the example of my list:

Band: The Red Jumpsuit Apparatus
    Song: *Face Down*
    Primary Emotion Attached: Anger
    Secondary Emotions Attached: Unworthy, embarrassed, insecure, and intimidated
    Notes: *Coincidentally, this is the song that started this journey for me. While driving home from my therapist's office, this song came on the radio. The emotions that coursed through me were uncontrollable. I had zero ability to turn off the tears or anger that zoomed like the speed of light from one end of my body to the other. It was instant. Instant anger, rage, sadness, and tears.

Band: Linkin Park
    Song: *A Place for my Head* *However, the entire Meteora, Hybrid Theory, and Minutes to Midnight albums helped me through some very rough years, so they remain a favorite to this day.

    Primary Emotion Attached: Sadness
    Secondary Emotions Attached: Anger, rage, insecurity
    Notes: Intense feelings of sadness almost immediately. Questioning why others have everything, and I am always

"left out." Why does everything seem easy for everyone else? I seem to have Murphy's law sitting on my shoulder.

BAND: The Cranberries
Song: *Ode to my Family*
Primary Emotion Attached: Sadness
Secondary Emotions Attached: Alone, hurt, and worthless
Notes: An intense longing for family, wanting somewhere to belong, wanting to feel loved. Everyone had great families (on the outside), and I didn't. I just wanted someone to "see" me.

BAND: Eminem
Song: *Lose Yourself*
Primary Emotion Attached: Anger
Secondary Emotion Attached: Fired up
Notes: This song made me instantly angry at my situation and fired me up to do something to change it. I want better, I deserve better, and I am willing to fight for better.

BAND: Andra Day
Song: *Rise Up*
Primary Emotion Attached: Happiness
Secondary Emotions Attached: Excited, fired up, motivated.

Notes: This song instantly makes me feel like I can do and be anything. I immediately think of my children and how I would move mountains for them.

. . .

NOW I CAN GO on and on with my list, honestly, and I have not uncovered all of the songs that I have some sort of memory attached to. To be honest, I'd say I have uncovered about 80%, but this list is constantly changing. We add new layers of our knot ball pretty much daily, and sometimes there are additional sensory stimuli attached to those memories. Once we learn to identify this, though, it is easier to deal with them almost immediately rather than let them sit and fester into a thick layer on your knot ball, eventually being buried by subsequent layers.

SO, take out that notebook I asked you to use for the work in this book and get to writing. Do not just rely on your memory. Pull up Pandora, YouTube, Amazon Music, Spotify, whatever your listening choice is, and listen to the music and listen to your feelings. Note down everything you are feeling along with the band or artist name, song title, and any primary and secondary emotions that you can pinpoint and move on. Do not try to figure out why this music makes you feel a certain way. Just note it, acknowledge it, and move on to the next piece of music. It is OK if you can only identify a few. Honestly, it is. Once we start working with those few songs and you get those layers removed, more will come flooding in because you have opened the floodgates, so to speak, and then you just start this process again. Identify, name, note, acknowledge, and move on.

I HOPE you're listening to music and making notes.

I AM SERIOUS. This is important, so don't be a rule breaker!

. . .

Do it now.

OK, I trust that you've done your homework and you have a list of one to a million songs. So now, what do we do with these songs, emotions, and memories, and how does all of this connect to this knot ball of shit? Well, it's actually quite simple in theory. The songs layer with the emotions to create the memories that typically you cannot remember, and so we will use the songs to evoke the emotions which created the memory in order to remove the negative connection or rewrite it altogether.

So, we are going to veer off here for one second and loop back to chapter one (sorry, this is just how my brain works). So, there are just three centers of your brain that I want you to concern yourself with. That's it, just three. In the back, near the base of your skull, is where you can imagine that your negative knot ball of shit is, like one of those circle ring magic toys that link with the other circle ring.

When we listen to music, our brains instantly take us not only back to our memories but also to the feelings attached to the memories. This is insanely significant because we are trying to get to or find the emotions that are attached to the memories that we cannot see or recognize because our brain hid them from us. Remember that tidbit from chapter one— the brain hides from us what it feels is damaging to us so we don't ever really know what is off or how to locate it. We only know something is off but never really what.

But hold up, wait a minute. Don't you want to know more about what we are doing, why we are doing it, and how it all works? Have no fear, my friend. We are going to go into that right now. Everything you could ever want to know about why this works and the specific areas of the mind we are working with incoming. Hold on tight, folks, it's about to get boring...I mean interesting...interesting!

NOW, LET'S DIG DEEP AND GET TO THE REAL WORK...YOU CAN DO IT!

"*I* play my game, my desperate pretending game, with a facade of assurance without and a trembling child within. So begins the glittering but empty parade of masks, and my life becomes a front." - Charles C. Finn

I KNOW...*le sigh*... more work to do, dude. If I could never work another day in my life, I wouldn't. But alas, here we are, ready and willing to put in the work for ourselves.

I trust that you gathered the needed items for this chapter. But first a word of caution...dun dun dunnnnnnnnnnn.

***I strongly urge you to only read through the principles of this at the moment, really only "going through the motions," if you will. You will need information from chapter 11 to close out a session from Chapter 10. So please, please, please read all of chapters 11 and 10 before you start.

Now that you have your song, and you know what you're focusing on (finding the emotions), all that's left is playing the music and "let it go...let it go...can't hold me back anymore." Right, well, almost. We need to get the simple rhythmic tapping down that will help us move the blockages.

For those of you who read chapter 4 (not needed), we will be giving a very brief overview of some of the things in that chapter. This is only because we certainly don't *need* to know everything there is to know about EMDR, the brain, and what we are doing, but we do need to have some sort of background and knowledge of these things so we can move forward. I also strongly urge you to create a playlist of two songs (your angry/sad song and your happy/feel-good song) before you sit down to get started. You won't want the interruption of changing music, and you just want to try to stay in the flow.

The tapping is going to be a needed part of what we are doing.

This simple technique was pioneered by Dr. Francine Shaperio, and it's called Eye Movement Desensitization Therapy, or EMDR for short, and it has revolutionized therapy for many people. EMDR rapidly gained popularity across the nation and quickly became the mode of choice for not only practitioners but also clients due to the relatively quick results.

EMDR typically focuses on trauma, and I know that many of you are thinking, "I don't have trauma, so what would I need this therapy for?" I get it. Being classified with trauma is scary, but think for one second back to two-year-old you. Do you think that the information that "daddy doesn't want me" is traumatic? Yes, odds are high that your brain classified this as a trauma.

Trauma is what causes our inner child, our authentic self, to be rejected and hidden, as it can no longer function in the world honestly. Instead, we use coping mechanisms we pick up from society, such as "suck it up," "don't cry," "be strong," and "get over it." As we grow up, we create barriers between our authentic selves and the world. These are masks that allow us to function in the world. They are meant to protect us from harm and hurt. Unfortunately, the suppression of the inner child can have serious consequences, especially if we have experienced significant traumas in our early lives.

EXAMPLES OF TRAUMA ARE ABUSE, neglect, abandonment, tragic events, enmeshment (which is living in a family without emotional boundaries), lack of approval, affection, attention, etc.

LET me elaborate a little bit so that we can gain a better understanding. When the brain interprets a trauma, it puts it in one of two categories:

1) an immediate danger that must be warned against all the time. We typically see this in PTSD sufferers as they "relive" their trauma in every facet of their lives and cannot get away from it. This normally happens in adulthood and makes a huge impact on the sufferer's life.

2) an incident that is extremely damaging and harmful. The brain hides it from you in order to protect you. We typically see this in everyday people who suffer from anxiety, depression, or a variety of mental disorders who can't quite "put the finger on" where it stems from. These events typically happen in childhood and leave a long-lasting impression on not only the child but also the adult's activities as well.

READING THROUGH THOSE TWO DESCRIPTIONS, I bet you were thinking, "Huh. Maybe, just maybe," and you're probably right. The vast majority of people suffer from brain-perceived trauma from their childhood, and they aren't even aware. Trauma is not always "arm falling off" or an event like 9/11. The brain can and often does (especially as a baby and young child when the brain is still building your storehouse of information) categorize things in a way that will have logical you scratching your head, saying, "What the heck?"

IT'S KIND OF like when someone comes into your kitchen and reorganizes everything or puts things back in the wrong place. You are left wondering out loud, "Who would put that there?" and "Where in the heck are the tongs?"

Your brain doesn't always make sense in the ways it does things. In fact, it rarely does. In terms of the brain, we know next to nothing about how it works, why some people respond differently to the same stimuli, or why some people are wired differently. I wish I could tell you that the geniuses are working on it, but they are not really. Because of the complexity of the brain, we can't really ask "broad" questions. When doing scientific research, we ask smaller questions that can fit into the broader question. Oftentimes, however, asking and answering that smaller question opens a can of worms that we were not necessarily prepared for, and we end up with more questions than answers. So, just know, your brain doesn't have to make sense to logical you. It likely never will, and your job is to figure out how to work within and with the illogical to live the best life possible.

So, back to trauma, yes, it is likely that at some point in your life, your brain classified some piece of information as trau-matic and therefore filed it as such, and it has been shaping your entire life from that moment on. We don't need to understand why our brain did this. We are just going to work with it.

So, EMDR and the tapping or eye movements that are associated with it are vital for "moving" the "hold-over" memories that we keep replaying or that are laying the "film" over new memories from processing to sorting and lastly to their final destination, whether that be long-term or short-term memory or the trash bin.

When EMDR first got its start, a lighted bar that your eyes followed was used to trigger the brain into letting go of the "film" it's been holding onto. Having the bilateral eye movements was a key component to the treatment working and people gaining quicker than average relief. However, this has evolved into a myriad of things that can be used in its place. Recent studies have discovered that it doesn't matter what the bilateral movement is, so long as there is bilateral movement. Studies have been done to see if EMDR was as effective without the bilateral stimuli, and just know that EMDR is more effective with the bilateral movement. And because we are using music to get to the feelings/emotions behind the memory, it only makes sense that you tap a comfortable beat with your hands or tap one with your feet. You could use any other method of bilateral movements that you find comfortable. It's honestly a personal preference.

For myself, I generally start out tapping a rhythm on myself somewhere to give my conscious mind some busy work and then move into just moving my eyes back and forth behind my closed eyelids. But as is our mantra throughout this whole book, there is no right or wrong way. What may work for me may not work for you. You may go through the steps below a few times and then modify them in a way that is more comfortable for you. That is OK. The key here is not following the script (although it is vital you don't skip a step) but putting in the work.

So, what exactly are we going to be doing with music, bilateral movements, and this thing called EMDR? I'm about to lay it all out for you.

You'll notice a lot of the techniques we will be doing are modified from existing EMDR therapy. This is not to diminish what we are doing or say this way is better. This is just so you, an individual, can practice this at home. If you feel that you would better benefit from a practitioner/client setting, please refer to the reference section in the back for ways to find a qualified EMDR practitioner near you.

So, let's get down to the brass tacks. This is the method that has worked for me, but also what I've fine-tuned through the help of my mentors and research to help people be able to use this effectively at home with great success.

Before we begin, find a free music site or create a playlist on Youtube (there are some great tutorials on it if you need one), and take your first negative/angry song and then your first happy/feel-good song and have them play one after the other so that you won't have to stop where you are in the process, you can just flow from one to the other seamlessly without distraction or disruption. This is kind of important, actually. You are emptying space from where the negative layer of the knot ball used to be. If you just all willy-nilly break concentration to start your happy/feel-good song, you may get distracted and never get to the happy/feel-good song. Can you imagine what can and will flood into that now empty space if you don't purposely fill it will something first? You'll just continue to be on this cosmic hamster wheel of repeating the said situations/events/people/feelings over and over if you don't select with purpose. So, for the sake of the hamster wheel (it's getting quite old by now, I'd imagine), just create a playlist so you don't have an interruption, and I promise it's super easy.

NOW THAT YOU'VE got your playlist primed to hit play, walk through exactly what you will be doing in a once-a-week session.

FIRST, I want you to start out with a self-hug. I know it sounds kind of silly, but in all honesty, you likely don't think too highly of yourself, so a hug won't hurt, and it may help. Before you begin to play any of your negative music, I want you to wrap your arms around yourself and just be with each hand lightly gripping the opposite upper arm. Slowly begin to tap out a beat on your upper arm with your fingers. It is OK if you begin to sway or rock slightly. It's also OK if you begin to feel your eyes move with you to the beat you are tapping. Just continue on with the tapping of the beat.

Take yourself to a safe space in your mind. Create your idyllic place. For me, that is a farm/ranch way out in the redwood forest. People cannot be seen or heard, and I am in my own little world out there. For you, it may be a tropical beach with a coconut drink. Wherever is safe for you, take yourself there. Allow yourself to just be there in this safe space. Focus on your feelings and notice how calm you are. Now there is no fear here. Know that you are completely and fully at ease and safe.

Once you're in this safe space and you are rating yourself below a four on the scale (*Using the Validity of Cognition or the Subjective Units of Distress Scales both found in Chapter 4 under Phases three through six, page 52*), you're ready to start your music. Remember, this is the place you will come back to, and you need to feel 100% at ease, safe, and comfortable here. There are no monsters under the bed here, no bad guys behind a tree. You are safe and in control here.

While still in your hug and tapping a rhythm, you can begin to play the angry music that you've selected to start with.

Don't force anything.

Just be present.

You are a silent observer on the journey your mind will take you on.

Just relax and let whatever comes forward come.

It's important to note what you're feeling.

You don't need to direct or try to decipher anything that is going on that you may be feeling or that you could get a glimpse of.

Just be present.

As you are going through physical cues, emotional responses, or imagery, just be present with them and move on when your brain shows you something new.

Just be present.

If at any time you're feeling too anxious, release yourself from it and come right back to your safe space.

Once you notice that your angry song is coming close to an end, begin to shift into your safe space.

Continue the tapping and your hug.

Know that you are safe and in control here.

When your happy/feel good music is playing, direct your mind to feeling happy.

Feel at peace.

Begin repeating your chosen mantra for the week. (Don't worry we will get to this deeply in our next chapter, I just wanted to cover what it would look like for you from start to finish)

Repeat your mantra at least three times.

When your happy/feel-good song is coming to an end, repeat the following mantra:

I am sorry.

Please forgive me.

I forgive you.

I love you.

Thank you.

*You can only listen to your positive song one time here. It is not necessary to listen to it multiple times. However, I often like the power of three, so I listen to three different positive songs after the one negative song. This serves to "run over" the negative song with a positive feeling (and mantras) many times over.

AFTER THE SONG list is over, I will quickly write in my book what I saw, felt, or any physical things that I felt.

I then move through my week. I play my happy/good feeling song regularly (normally 3-5 times a day) and jot in my notebook anything that happens. Typically, this includes things like how many times I "yell" stop, what triggered that, and how I felt during the process.

RIGHT BEFORE YOU start your next session, you will review your past week and review the song from your last session. If there is any lingering pain or issues when playing the song, use that song again this week in your session. Note again how you're feeling about it on the scale, along with any feelings, memories, or items you can surrounding the emotion.

If you show or feel no response to the song, great job. You are ready to move on to the next one. You're no longer holding on to the negative emotion that you attached significance to through the song. You can now move on to another song, emotion, and mantra to focus on.

KEEP REPEATING this process until you've worked through all of your songs. You can always re-evaluate your songs and emotional attachment to them at any time. This is one of the reasons I suggested keeping it all in one notebook. You can easily go back to the start of your journey and see how far you've come or have a list to re-evaluate at any time.

LET'S take an example again so we can see how this would look.

I begin with my hug and tapping. I take myself to my safe space, ensuring that I am relaxed, comfortable, and safe.

When I am ready, I begin to invoke the desired emotion through my angry music.

I first feel it in my heart. It feels heavy, not painful, but extremely weighted down so that it's cumbersome or a burden.

My mind flies next to an aunt, and this doesn't make sense. I simply note it and continue on.

I then see a crying baby, the isolation, loneliness, and need I feel coming from the baby are very real. I feel them in every ounce of my being. I hurt for this child, and I instinctively want to pick up the baby and give it some comfort.

My song is coming to an end.

I begin to focus on the tapping and the feelings of the present.

I bring myself to my safe space while my happy song begins to play.

In my safe space with my happy song, I repeat my mantra. "I am loving, and I give my love freely."

When my happy song is coming to an end, I repeat the following mantra:

I am sorry.
Please forgive me.
I forgive you.
I love you.
Thank you.

AND THAT'S IT. Now I know a lot of you are thinking, "this is a lot of work, this is going to take a lot of time." Well, yes and no. Humans tend to make things more complicated than they are. We like to keep the status quo, even if the status quo is not for our greatest good. When we are stuck in that dead-end job that we know will not go anywhere, we do it because we are afraid to step outside the status quo. We let that fear conquer us. Those "what if's" keep playing the game they always do in your brain, running a million and one scenarios to tell you all the reasons why you should stay where you are. This is like that. The brain is happy to be in what it knows, what it's comfortable with. It has created this world for you, and it's quite pleased with itself. It certainly does not want to buck the system.

So, it seems relatively simple on paper, as things often do, but in application, well...

Right now, you are not really in tune with your body, feelings, and emotions. As you progress, you will be. It will come easier and more naturally for you to self-correct. The process is initially semi-cumbersome. It's not as easy as, say, breathing, but it's a damn sight easier than the SATs. The biggest problem I see for many people is commitment. They can do it for a few days...then life happens, and they forget. Self-care is why this should be your top priority every day. If you are not taking care of yourself, who will?

Honestly, this entire process takes me less than fifteen minutes in the morning. I choose to do this both at night before bed and first thing in the morning. I choose to start my day knowing how awesome and capable I am, and I choose to end my day ensuring that nothing crept into my day that doesn't need to be there. I was once like you, wondering where on earth I was going to find thirty minutes in my day, and then I realized I could not move forward without taking care of myself. I had to find any time I need to be able to shake free from this brain-drain road that I was on and move to something better for me.

So, yes, it is work. No, it does not take much time. And yes, this is a need because you are worth every second you invest in yourself.

LET'S FOCUS ON FILLING THAT EMPTY SPACE

So, you did your dry run. How was it? Did it feel weird? I'm betting that it wasn't at all like you were anticipating, and you're probably thinking this will be fairly easy to implement on a daily basis.

And you're right, it is. While it will require focus and maybe a reminder alarm for the first two weeks, it is pretty easy compared to a lot of the other things out there for you.

So, if you read chapter 4, then you are already aware that we need to fill the empty space we just created with something because if we don't...well, the old shit will just flood right back in, or worse, new bad shit, and we will be right back to square one. Clinicians who administer EMDR call this the Installation Phase, and really this just means putting positive information in the previous bad information space.

But how do we know what positive information we should put in there?

. . .

AHHH, good question, and it's one where we are going to turn once again to music! WOOT WOOT!

This is a theme in my life. I really turn to music for a lot of things, and this is no exception.

JUST LIKE YOU found the music that makes you feel ragey, angry, sad, teary, whatever those negative emotions are, now you are going to find some positive emotional songs. Oh, yeah. I mean, who doesn't like to find and listen to some absolutely awe-inspiring music that makes you feel good and happy?

If you were paying attention back when I was listing my example negative emotion songs, you would have noticed that I slipped one of my motivational songs in there as an example.

It's OK. You can go back and look. I won't tell on you.

Did you find it?

See, I told you.

We are pretty much just going to do the same thing we did in Chapter 10, but now we are going to find all those happy feelings and good songs. We are going to work this the same exact way. Find a song list of for primary positive emotions and secondary emotions we notice. So, it will look like this.

BAND: Andra Day

Song: *Rise Up*

Primary Emotion Attached: Happiness

Secondary Emotion Attached: Excited, fired up, motivated

Notes: This song instantly makes me feel like I can do and

be anything. I immediately think of my children and how I would move mountains for them.

BE careful here when you are making your list. It is very easy to feel "fired up," for example, in both a positive and negative way. We don't want to attach any negative connotations with these song choices, so really analyze them to ensure you are laying the right tune, so to speak.

I'VE CREATED a list to help navigate you if you're feeling stuck. If these speak to you, great, grand, wonderful. Use them as a jumping-off point. If they don't really speak to you, then look deeper into what makes you happy and brings you joy so you can find your list.

MY RULE of thumb is you need three songs or roughly eight to ten minutes of positive music for every negative song. (Don't worry, we will go through what to do with all this in a minute, I promise) but it's not necessary. You can be successful just by playing your positive song one time, and it is my personal preference and rule of thumb to play roughly three after I listen to my negative music. There is no cookie-cutter version of this that will fit everyone. Some people may discover they only need to play the song once and only a few times during the week to be successful, while others may need three+ songs immediately following the negative one and listen to nothing but positive music during the week. We are all wired differently; there is no one size fits all solution for people. You have to do the legwork to find the right mix for you.

· · ·

AIN'T NO MOUNTAIN HIGH ENOUGH – Marvin Gaye & Tammi Terrell

GET UP STAND UP — Bob Marley

IT'S MY LIFE — Bon Jovi

YOU GOTTA BE — Des Ree

WE ARE THE CHAMPIONS — Queen

IMAGINE — John Lennon

DON'T WORRY BE HAPPY — Bobby McFerrin

HERE COMES THE SUN — The Beatles

STAND By Me -- Ben E. King

FREEDOM — Pharrell Williams

HALL OF FAME — The Script Ft. Will.i.am

. . .

HIGH HOPES — Panic at the Disco

WONDER — Natalie Merchant

THE MIDDLE — Jimmy Eat World

THESE ARE ALL ACTUALLY on my playlist that is titled "Everyday Motivation." I use this playlist when I am doing a session on myself and as a pick-me-up when needed. I typically play my "Everyday Motivation" at least once a day. If it's a super stressful or trying day, I may listen to nothing but this playlist all day.

REMEMBER when I said I work ungodly hours six days a week? Yeah, that's at like 3 am getting up at 2:30 am. Naps are unheard of for me, so I go from about 2:30 am to 9-10 pm daily. I don't stop. Some days while writing this book (or for my other job), I need that motivation to kick me square in the butt, so I get it done instead of binging *The Magicians* on Netflix or something. So, I play my "Everyday Motivation" playlist to get me pumped and to also remind me that I can do this, it is bigger than me, and I have to get it done. (I told you, I still got issues, but I am less of a hot mess most days.)

BACK TO YOUR LIST. Once you have your positive motivation list, make sure you write down the emotions you feel with your specific songs (these are important. We are getting to the why. Be patient) because we are going to use those positive emotions to create your new mantra for the week.

145

. . .

YES, you should only do one session focusing on the negative music and emotions on yourself a week. Period. Full. Stop. I've said it before, and I will say it again. Only one session a week. You don't want to overload your brain. Ideally it would look like this...

Monday- *do Negative Feeling/emotion session immediately followed by your positive music playlist. - Play this positive music playlist as many times as needed throughout the day. Repeat positive mantra as many times as needed throughout the day.*

Tuesday - **Saturday**- *Play the positive music playlist as many times as needed throughout the day. Repeat positive mantra as many times as needed throughout the day.*

Sunday- *reflect on your week and how you're feeling. You may need to repeat the same mantra/song/feelings or you may be able to move on to something new.**

So, just like in chapter ten, when we identified our negative core beliefs and our related secondary belief patterns, we are going to do the same for positive belief patterns that directly combat the negative belief pattern we are trying to resolve. Pretty cool, right?

So, your list should look like this.

BAND: The Script Ft. Will.i.am
    Song: *Hall of Fame*
    Primary Positive Emotion: Happy
    Secondary Positive Emotions: Excited, fired-up, passionate

Notes: This song makes me feel like I can do anything. I can feel the positive energy flowing to me.

BAND: Panic at the Disco
   Song: *High Hopes*
   Primary Positive Emotion: Happy
   Secondary Positive Emotions: Elated, excited, and motivated
   Notes: This song is reminiscent of the 90's songs. I feel like this song was written directly for me. Every note and word was plucked out of my life and given a lyrical nature.

You get the general idea of how to construct these because it's the exact same way we did it a few chapters ago.

A NOTE ON POSITIVE EMOTIONS: be really careful that you are not mistaking negative feeling good for positive feeling good. You are maybe wondering what I am talking about. I explain best with examples, so, onward we go to another awesome example.

So, I feel super awesome when I play songs like Korn's *Shoots and Ladders*, anything by Tool, or Rage Against the Machine. These songs don't hold any negative connotations for me, and I genuinely like the music. But these songs also don't bring any positive feelings. They don't make me happy, and they don't make me feel loved; they don't bring my mood up; in fact, sometimes quite the opposite happens. I often call this music my calm down music. When I am upset, I will normally plug my iPod into my car, select an artist from above (or one similar), and listen to the music as loud as possible in my car until I feel better.

So, when selecting your positive music, really evaluate if it is positive or negative positive.

Now let's take a look at those positive affirmations that we also need in this stage.

THESE FALL in line with your core negative belief pattern. So, grab the notebook you've been using throughout this book and flip back to the negative core beliefs you wrote down. Find the one that is most troubling to you. Now when I say most troubling to you, it likely won't be the first one you want to select. It will probably be the one you want to avoid, like the plague. If you're not ready to start there, that it OK. Remember, there is no right or wrong way. Just pick the one you are comfortable with working on and start there.

Now that you have your negative core belief you want to start working on, you're going to find the positive affirmation you are going to say the entire week. (Remember, one session a week)

Only choose one affirmation that you are going to keep in your mind all week. Don't try to "layer" the affirmations on top of each other because, quite frankly, you likely won't remember, and then you will likely beat yourself up over forgetting the affirmations that you were supposed to remember. (I've been here and done that. Not fun. I am trying to save you from setbacks and failures and give you the straightest path to awesome.)

EVERY TIME you have a setback in your old behavior or thought pattern, say "Stop" silently in your head. Actually, I pretty much yell this. I feel like I need to because I am trying to grab the attention of the mega superhighway of shit that I am unhappily, yet obviously traveling down while listening to my angsty music that fuels the fire of shit. You may have to "yell" more than a few times to actually get your brain's attention. It's accustomed to just running on autopilot and you not really bothering it or making waves. It's kind of "in the zone," and you may need to nudge it more than a few times. I can promise that the first time you yell, "Stop", and your brain actually listens, you're going to be a little amazed.

After you have the attention of the brain, redirect it with a positive yet true affirmation. You can select any one that you feel will work best, but I encourage you to stick with the linked belief patterns.

But (there is literally always a but), remember back in chapter 1 when we talked about "truth-telling" to our brain? Essentially, if it isn't a "known" truth for us, the manager will throw it straight into the bin, and it will never get to the CEO, and we will never be able to truly impart that new "truth" we want to so very badly.

Yeah, that shit sucks.

But we have a workaround, if you remember.

We simply tell the manager an undeniable truth that he has to pass on to the CEO. DONE-ZO!

Remember, you do not have to use any of the affirmations I provide here. If you can come up with one that is more fitting for your life and circumstances, then more power to you. I don't want to be the end all, be all for this. I want to be the jumping-off point that gives you an idea, a path, and then you run with it and spread it like gangbusters.

So, if you want to make your own affirmations for this, there are some things to keep in mind.

Keep it short. One sentence. Preferably under ten words. You need to be able to remember this at every moment of the day. You seriously won't have time to try to remember what PEMDAS means in your cryptic mind. You'll honestly revert back to your old train of thought that you're trying to get rid of if this new affirmation is not easily remembered and on the tip of your tongue.

Use creative words. You didn't pick up this book (or the fifteen others on your bookshelf) because you have stellar self-esteem and think you are just the bees-knees, so we have to get creative here. I tend to use things like "unique" for "weird" (which people call me weird all the time. Believe me, there's not a damn thing wrong with it) or "great to be alive." Some other words to consider are; grateful, magical, creative, interested, optimistic, animated, tenacious, and ambitious.

a word of caution try to stay away from words like; content, flattered, fortunate, good, and hopeful. These words won't really help you on this journey, so just toss them straight into the bin. I had some people ask me why I don't like these words and why I don't use them in mantras, and I'd like to address that. Most of these are either fake positive or have underlying negative connotations to them. For example, **Fortunate** implies that you are favored over someone else. **Good** is the answer we give everyone when we don't want to say how we are really feeling. **Content** is stagnant, you are content with life meaning you don't want it to change. **Flattered** depends on someone else's perception of you and it can be both negative and positive. **Hopeful** means it may never come but you are hopeful it might.

Lastly, try everything to connect the two core beliefs (the negative and the positive) in the one affirmation. For example, if I am working on "I am worthless," I would say something like, "I enjoy being so animated, full of life, and creative." You cannot deny these facts if they are true to you and something you enjoy. So, get creative with your truth-telling. Connect some positive truth (that is undeniable) to counteract the negative.

IF YOU'RE NOT REALLY into all of that creative stuff and just want me to lay out some new truths for you to follow, read on, my friends, I have some good ones for you.

CORE BELIEF ~ I am worthless

NEW CORE AFFIRMATION ~ I appreciate my unique life

While this may seem like not much of a positive affirmation, it is reaffirming that you are amazing and unique. You can also use something like…

I have done a lot of awesome things in my life.

I can do great things today.

What an amazing day, I will enjoy it.

I am grateful for this day.

I am fun, fun-loving, and creative.

CORE BELIEF ~ I am powerless

New Core Affirmation ~ I remember, I trust myself.

This one is really powerful. You are giving everything back to yourself, and you are allowing yourself to accept that you *are* in control and are powerful. You can also use something like…

I am open to trusting myself.

I am worthy of life.

I honor my true self and highest good.

I walk with faith and belief in who I am.

CORE BELIEF ~ I am wrong/unsure

New core affirmation ~ I trust my inner wisdom and intuition; it guides me.

Trust is a big thing, and often, we do not trust ourselves to be in tune enough to know we are doing the right thing.

Placing trust back into yourself will allow you to take back control and shake the "unsure" in your life. You can also use something like...

I trust myself to make the best decision for me.

I know my inner wisdom guides me to the right decisions.

I let go of worries and thoughts that drain me.

I seek a new way of thinking about a situation/thing/feeling/person (you can put an actual name, event, or situation in here. Example: I seek a new way of thinking about Tommy).

CORE BELIEF ~ I am defective/not right

New core affirmation ~ I fully approve of who I am, even as I get better.

You are leaving the door open here for more amazingness to come. We are not saying, "I am perfect right now with no flaws." We are saying, "I accept myself, flaws and all, and I will get better." You can also use something like this...

I am a good person.

I am a unique child of this world.

I am a radiant and joyous person.

Life is filled with joy, happiness, and wonder, and it surrounds me.

CORE BELIEF ~ I am nothing/I don't exist

New core affirmation ~ I am confident in my individuality

This lets the brain know we are OK being exactly who we are. We don't care if we are unique; we like it, and so do others. You can also use something like...

I may be one in seven billion...but I am also *one* in seven billion.

I take the time to show my friends I care about them.

I am more than good enough, and I get better every day.

I am authentic, true, and expressive.

CORE BELIEF ~ I am unlovable/unwanted

New core affirmation ~ I am beautiful and smart, and that's how everyone around me sees me.

Likely, there are more than a few people who secretly envy you and think you're just the bee's knees. This will allow you to be open to see how others see you, which is a good thing. You can also use something like...

I approve of the person I am becoming.

I love myself and others unconditionally.

I am an authentic person, and others see that.

I am grateful for my life and those in it.

ONCE YOU GET into the groove of reminding your brain of your new path at every opportunity, it will prove to be a hard habit to break.

SAY WHAT?

I KNOW I *just* told you it's easier to get on your super mega highway of shit and keep on keeping on with what you've been doing. But once you start yelling, "Stop" to your brain, it does stand up and pay attention. It will remember that. And each time you try to fall back into your old pattern, you'll not only remember "stop" a lot easier, but you'll also find your brain a lot more receptive. So, when you first start yelling. "Stop" to yourself, it may (and likely will) take a few (or more than a few) times of yelling at yourself for your brain to notice you're directing that command at it.

YOU WILL NEVER BELIEVE how good it feels and how quickly you start responding to it. Do you know how good it feels to one day realize, as you're jamming out to your ah-mazing "Motivation Playlist," that you actually feel good? There is no lie in there this time, and we're not "faking it until we make it." We are certainly no longer putting on a brave face or one of the many masks we are so used to wearing...we really feel good. It is such a powerful feeling.

So, I have probably quite literally confused the hell out of you.

The workings of my brain are just as mysterious as yours, and this is how my brain works. I will not apologize for that because it makes me totally unique, and you've stuck with me this far.

So...

LET'S break this *whole* thing down from start to finish so you can connect my brain's dots.

1: Identify negative core music, feelings, and emotions.
2: Link your emotions to music that resonates with you.
3: Identify positive core music, feelings, and emotions.

4: Link your positive emotions to positive music that resonates with you.

5. Find or create your new positive affirmation for the week. Try to have it connect with your initial negative and your final positive feelings.

6. Take out your notebook and write down any and all initial notions you have about the song, feelings, or emotions you are trying to target. Remember to rate your feelings on the subject using the scales provided and be brutally truthful. No lying to yourself with some "this isn't so bad" bullcrap. Lying to yourself will only slow your healing and keep you right where you are. Remember, it's OK to recognize the nasty crap from your past. It's OK to bring it to light, as long as you recognize it for what it is (nasty crap), and *let it go*. It's not serving you in any way, holding it so tightly to you as you've been.

7. Move into your safe space, tapping/moving rhythmically at a speed that is comfortable to you. Stay in your space, knowing you are completely safe, nothing can harm you here, and you are in complete control.

8. Play negative music while continuing the tapping/moving rhythmically at a speed that is comfortable for you.

9. Allow your brain to "go." Have your starting negative emotion place and just follow where your brain takes you until the song(s) go off.

10. Immediately go into your "safe space" of positive music, feelings, and emotions. You can play this for three times the length of the negative song, but it's not needed. Remember you will be cementing this positive/happy/feel-good song/feeling all week. Allow your brain to go but gently guide it only to positive things until the song's end.

11. Take out your notebook again and write down everything you can remember. Both good and bad. Note it all.

Make sure to include your music choices and your affirmation of choice if you need to return to it later as much as you can detail what you feel. Remember to rate your feelings on this subject using the scales provided.

12. Continue to listen to your music at least once a day and practice the "Stop" and redirect method any time you need to. You can and should document when you need to throughout the week.

13. After one week, come back to the initial song. Taking out your notebook, write down how you feel about this song now, and the emotions that are/were tied to it. Make sure to use the scales provided so you can accurately compare how you felt before and how you're feeling now.

14. If your feelings are still pretty bad regarding this, re-do this method targeting the same song/feelings/emotions. My rule of thumb is anything over a four, and I do it again. If your feelings have moved below a four and you're ready, move to the next one on your list that you're ready to tackle. Continue to repeat the steps. Continue to write down any changes in your notebook.

SEE, now this doesn't look too daunting, does it? It's really just listening to music and writing things down, and it's easy, like Sunday morning.

When you focus on emptying the negative space that has been taking up residency in your brain and altering every event you can begin to remember, you "undo" the knot ball of shit. Then you process the memories as they should have been, replacing that negative space with positive space, and you do all this using a medium that has been around as long as written history has been. And when it's written like that, it sounds like "magic," but make no mistake that you will have to put in the work here. You will have to be diligent with your feelings to "catch" them throughout the week. You will have to get a notebook to write down what you're feeling and actually *look* at it. (I know, humans don't really like to evaluate things that disturb them because then, you know, we have to deal with them.) You'll have to carve thirty minutes for yourself once a week to go through the music therapy and be honest with yourself about how you are doing. You will have to listen to your chosen "happy" music at least three times a day. If you don't do these things, it won't work. Are the tasks simple? Yes. Will our brain make every excuse in the book for keeping the status quo that it created and, quite frankly, it likes? Yes. Will this take effort on your part to stop going with the flow and take control? Yes. But you can do it. (If you read that in Rob Schneider's voice, you're my kind of people.)

Now, if you're looking for this to take minimal time, I am sorry to tell you that it likely won't.

While you will begin to feel better pretty much right away, and this is mainly because you're pumping your brain full of feel-good music and our feel-good mantra, you will really notice the change when the negative music no longer has a hold on you. You'll be able to listen to your previously held "negative music" without marking it on the Validity of the Cognition Scale. Those songs, and thereby those memories, will no longer hold negative emotions, memories, or feelings for you. It will just be another song in your playlist.

That is the end goal. To be able to hear that negative song and have zero emotion tied to it. It just becomes another song from your history that you can either listen to or not because that choice will now be yours. Previously, you may have avoided that song/music choice like the plague because you didn't *want* to stir up the negative that you subconsciously *knew* was tied to it. Once the emotional significance is undone, the song becomes just another song.

I have had people ask me to give them a timeline of when they should start feeling better, and, sadly, there is no concrete answer for this. Your layers of knot ball could be more tightly interwoven than Sally's. Sally could be listening to no other music besides her "everyday motivation" playlist. There are a whole host of variables that come into play. However, I can say that you should (if you are doing your homework and following the once-a-week and daily activities) start feeling better within two weeks.

You'll begin to notice the attitude shift in how you're carrying yourself, how you're behaving, how you're believing, and how you're interacting with everyone.

For the people who have done the process, and for me, they describe it as a "lighter" feeling, like weights you didn't know you were carrying are gone or significantly less. Some people reported that pains that they've had for as long as they can remember are gone or diminished. Remember that the negativity we are holding onto doesn't just harm us mentally; it breaks us down physically as well. Most people reported increased energy and motivation within the two-week span. They took that as their *sign* that this was working and that they needed to continue.

AND YOU'RE PRETTY MUCH ready to go. No joke this time, no more test runs. You are ready to start this journey for yourself. No one can really help you out of this hole but you, and now you have to get to work.

COMMON MISSTEPS, ISSUES, AND PROBLEMS. WE CAN FIX IT.

~

*W*e expect that "nothing comes easy" (even though that is entirely false. Tons of things come easy), but *man*, this makes me want to give up. Don't fret, and certainly do not give up. Let me say that louder for the people in the back. *Do not give up.*

DO NOT, under any circumstances, stop trying. All of the old mega superhighways that you have been painstakingly removing will come back with a vengeance and man, will you notice that.

I am not asking you to do this for me. I am asking you to do this for *you*.

DO NOT GIVE up on you.

YOU DESERVE BETTER.

. . .

YOU ARE BETTER.

SO, now that we are not going to give up, let's run through some of the more common pitfalls that I have experienced, seen, and had reported to me.

FEAR IS the number one issue or problem witnessed.

THAT DAMN "WHAT IF" game will screw you up.

FEAR HOLDS us tight in the spot we are in with a million little "what ifs" that wreak havoc on what you know is right.

Let's do an example (because if you have not noticed, I love them!). Say you're a first-year doctor, and you get offered a job where you currently live, but it's not in your field of experience, nor is it anywhere you want to be. Then you get offered a job across the country, at a place you've never been to, but it's in your field of experience, and it's totally the job you want. What do you do?

IF YOU'RE LIKE 90% of us, you'll hammer the decision to death, making yourself wrought with stress, worry, and panic, silently analyzing the decision a million ways to Sunday, only to decide "it's not for me."

IT IS TOTALLY FOR YOU, and you would have likely loved living in your new place, and you would have found a better and cheaper place to live, and on and on that goes.

. . .

So, why in the hell did you talk yourself out of this great opportunity?

THAT DAMN "WHAT IF" game played, and because your brain is oh so intelligent and thoughtful, it brought you every possible bad scenario it could think of, that you remember or not, from every person, television show, movie, book, or anything else relevant and displayed them all for you like they were possible in your life. (To read more about the brain/eye/sound trick, head to chapter 9. There are tons of details and studies there).

So, do your best to shut fear up!

SERIOUSLY, I could write an entire book on fear (and I just may), but for the purpose of this book, just shut it up.

EVEN IF IT IS SHORT-TERM.

EVENTUALLY, after you show fear who is boss, it will get quieter and quieter until it's only a faint memory in the back of your mind.

So, follow the same steps we practiced earlier.

. . .

TELL YOUR BRAIN TO STOP.

BE FIRM.

REDIRECT to what you are currently focusing on that week.

BE CONSISTENT. Follow through daily on not allowing fear to creep in.

FOLLOW through is number two (although it is tied into number one), and I got every excuse in the book.

GROWN ADULTS GIVING me the old "dog ate my homework" excuse because they didn't follow through.

BUT WHY?

IF YOU GUESSED FEAR, you are pretty smart, and you get a cookie for that.

YOU WILL LITERALLY FIND any and every excuse in the book to not do something, even if that something is in your better interest because your brain has no idea what is on the other side.

. . .

IT'S OVER THERE HAVING its own anxiety attack. "What will I do if there are no neuropathways?" "How will I get X, Y, Z done now?" And so on. Because, remember, every "truth" it has told you, it also believes. So, I get that you are unsure and scared. If you consciously know that something is in your better interest and there are a million and a half excuses on why you can't start or whatever, then do it anyway. Because, quite honestly, unless you are thinking of doing something that will threaten your life, health, or safety (or that of someone else), your brain is seriously just trying yo keep the status quo it has worked so long to build up.

I AM GOING to give you an example (I love them), and I will make it personal (hint, it's about me).

I HAVE ALWAYS LOVED to write and make up stories. Everyone told me I should, and I didn't.

EVERY SINGLE NEGATIVE thing I could ever imagine happening as a result of me publishing my own work was laid bare.

I SAT PARALYZED IN FEAR.

DAY AFTER DAY.

NEVER REALLY MOVING FORWARD because I couldn't. I was OK in the ok-ness of life.

. . .

AND THEN I started this year of *no fear*!
The single best decision I have ever made!

I HAVE JUMPED out of planes this year, you guys. I am terrified of heights!

I HAVE MOVED across the country. Somewhere that is very different from anywhere I have ever lived.

I HAVE TAKEN A NEW JOB. Not in my wheelhouse at all, although I enjoy the work.

I HAVE MADE NEW FRIENDS.

AND I ALLOWED myself to be me, including writing again and submitting it to publishing companies.

I NEVER THOUGHT I could do this, and fear kept me in the "what if" game.
Fear kept holding me back despite the fact that, at 17, I cold queried a publishing company with a book idea, a book I had not even written yet. They wrote back that they wanted to publish me. This was a Big 5 before you had to have an agent to get in the door. The "world" told me I was good enough, but fear told me all sorts of other things.

. . .

AND I BELIEVED that stupid nonsense for another 21 years. I believed every "truth" like it was gospel and kept myself in all sorts of situations that were not good for me.

THE "TRUTH" the brain tells you does not always have your best interest at heart.

THE "TRUTH" the brain tells you is meant to keep you in its version of safe that it has developed over your lifetime.

SIT AND WATCH SOME CHILDREN. They are some of the greatest examples of this. Some literally have no fear. They will climb as high as they can, without a thought or care about how they will get down, and they just know they want to see, be, do, and climb. I've sat and shushed my inner fear watching my youngest boy climb (he *loves* to climb). I have bitten my tongue to not project my fear onto him. If he thinks he can do it, who am I to tell him otherwise? Just because little Timmy fell down the well and Lassie was the only way to save him doesn't mean my boy will be the same. You cannot tamper with another human being with your own perceived fears that your brain has developed throughout your lifetime.

I HAVE WATCHED my son climb up and down many trees in his 13 years. I have watched him fearlessly "do" and enjoy every second of life and nature. His brain tells him something completely different from mine, and I cannot impose my brain's "truths" on him.

. . .

AND THAT'S REALLY what happens. Well-meaning parents, adults, caregivers, teachers, etc. all impose their brain's version of truth onto these young children, and if this young child is told enough times, that becomes their brain's truth, and the cycle will continue.

LIVE YOUR OWN TRUE TRUTH.

NOT SOME HOLLYWOOD, crazy perception of truth.

BECAUSE WE HAVE ALREADY ESTABLISHED that your brain is a liar, and while some of the time, it has your best intentions at heart, most of the time, it is really working off of other people's "truths" that have nothing to do with you.

RESOURCES, BECAUSE NOW I KNOW YOU WANT TO LEARN MORE

*S*o, there are tons of resources available if you want to learn more about EMDR, how music relates to *everything*, and how the brain is a big fat liar, and I am going to give you a road map to find them.

EMDR: Dr. Francine Shapiro is really the authority on EMDR. She is the pioneer, blazing trails where others thought it was hooey, and she continues to be the foremost source on EMDR, even in death. If you have questions about EMDR, I highly suggest *Getting Past Your Past: Take Control of Your Life with Self-Help Techniques from EMDR Therapy* by Dr. Francine Shapiro. This is one of the first books I bought on the subject, and it still has a prominent place on my bookshelf.

CHANGING YOUR BRAIN: Daniel G. Amen wrote *Change Your Brain Change Your Life,* and let me tell you, if you have not read it, add it to your must-read list. Daniel Amen uses

SPECT imaging to help patients revamp their entire brain mapping. He's written several books on the science of brain mapping and changing how we think.

NEURAL PATHWAYS: There are actually two books I would recommend if you're interested in learning more about neural pathways, how they work, and how to create new pathways. First, I would recommend *Self Directed Brain Change: Rewire Your Neural Pathways for Happiness and Resilience* by Rick Hanson, Ph.D. I listened to the audiobook of this, and let me tell you, it makes so much sense. Secondly, I would recommend *Limitless Mind* by Jo Boaler. Once you get your conscious mind wrapped around the fact that literally everything is possible, everything becomes so much easier.

FALSE MEMORIES: I highly recommend researching this further; however, most of the books are educational texts, which means they are not cheap. If you want to learn more and stretch your brain, I recommend *The Science of False Memory (Oxford Psychology Series)* by C.J. Brainerd and V. F. Reyna. Keep in mind this is a textbook, and that means it is at times dry and harder to read.

THE MUSIC BRAIN CONNECTION: I recommend *The Secret Language of the Heart* by Barry Goldstein. Mr. Goldstein really focuses on music in general and not necessarily tailored to the music that makes individual music soundtracks that we have playing in our lives. There are nuggets of amazing insight and a real foundation of understanding the link between music and our brain.

. . .

ANOTHER BOOK I recommend is *This is your Brain on Music - The Science of a Human Obsession* by Daniel J. Levitin. Again, this book doesn't necessarily focus on an individual musical soundtrack but on how the brain responds to music in general and how creating music can have both positive and negative effects on the brain. This book is well worth the read if you're interested in diving deeper into the connections that the brain makes.

IF YOU'RE interested in the awareness of life and its omnipresence around us (otherwise known as the law of attraction), there are a few books and authors I would recommend. First, I would recommend Pam Grout's *E-squared* (and the subsequent books that came from it) for the simple reason that it offers actual experiments to test the Universe and its ability to answer your requests. The beauty of those books is that even if you go into the experiments skeptical and wanting to prove the Universe wrong, you are still putting faith in the experiment, and by its own fulfillment, it will work. (Energy goes where energy flows, like attracts like, etc., etc., etc.)

NEXT, I would recommend Mike Dooley. I have been a student of working with my mind to achieve what I want for years (since at least 2007), and when I tell you nothing made more sense than his Matrix, I mean it! His book aptly titled *Playing the Matrix* is a game changer along with *Infinite Possibilities: The Art of Living your Dreams.* These are by far two books that won't leave my bookshelf, and I will always recommend them. I am an Infinite Possibilities certified trainer and enjoy helping the community as much as I can.

I WOULD ALSO RECOMMEND Mel Robbins. She has a way of getting you to act to live the life you want. So many times, we know what we need to do but can't quite make a move to act on it. She is a wonderful motivator in that respect. I would highly recommend the audiobooks if you can because hearing someone else tell you what you need to do just hits differently. Her books *The High Five Habit* and *The Five Second Rule* are standard practice in my house.

LASTLY IS another author who has a more scientific approach, and let me tell you, Lynne McTaggart is just amazing! The information she presents is astounding, and every time I read through her work or attend one of her workshops, I am always awe-inspired by the revelations. I would start off with her book *The Intention Experiment: Using Your Thoughts to Change Your Life and the World* simply due to the fact that the science within this book is mind-blowing.

IF YOU ARE LOOKING for local EMDR practitioners or resources, there are two websites that will direct you to practitioners in your area.
https://www.emdria.org/find-an-emdr-therapist/
https://www.psychologytoday.com/us/therapists/emdr

AFTERWORD

Resources, References, and going further down the rabbit hole

Not all the References used in this book, but A LOT of them. Most of the information is not directly quoted BUT is located in the resource section. This is simply the appendix of quoted things within this book for your ease and reference.

https://www.6seconds.org/2017/04/27/plutchiks-model-of-emotions/

https://en.wikipedia.org/wiki/Maslow%27s_hierarchy_of_needs

http://www.awaken.com/2018/07/levels-of-consciousness/

https://blog.bufferapp.com/connections-in-the-brain-understanding-creativity-and-intelligenceconnections
2-1   https://www.sciencedaily.com/releases/2017/04/170412181341.htm

2-2 The Secret Language of the Heart. Barry Goldstein. Pg xvi

8-2 Jon Lieff, "Music stimulates Emotions Though Specific Brain Circuits." http://jonlieffmd.com/blog/music-stimulates-emotions-through-specific-brain-circuits

7-1   https://www.sciencedaily.com/releases/2000/06/000601164617.htm

4-1   https://sciencing.com/the-functions-of-the-left-temporal-lobe-12214661.html

4-2   https://www.ncbi.nlm.nih.gov/pmc/articles/PMC3548359/#idm140038008667888title pages 8-9

4-3   https://www.ncbi.nlm.nih.gov/pmc/articles/PMC3548359/#idm140038008667888title pages 18-19

4-4   https://nba.uth.tmc.edu/neuroscience/m/s4/chapter06.html

4-5   https://staff.washington.edu/eloftus/Articles/sciam.htm

5-1   remember-where-you-were-on-911-study-suggests-memories-may-be-distorted

5-2 PMC2925254

ABOUT THE AUTHOR

MJ Nicholson is a partner, parent, and author who has a passion for helping others. MJ is also an international motivational speaker who often speaks about overcoming fear and writing.

As an executive life coach, MJ has experience helping entrepreneurs with ADHD cultivate success through micro habits. MJ also coaches others through the writing process so they can become published.

MJ has over 12 years of ghostwriting experience and is always looking to expand her skills. MJ teaches small groups of adults and children about infinite possibilities and the awesomeness of the Universe.

An avid learner, crafter, bibliophile, garden enthusiast, and travel lover MJ is often found outside or with her nose in a book. She is also an eternal optimist and cheerleader for others willing to help you reach your goal.

She loves mail and can be reached through her website www.wildemooncreative.com